THE FIRST TIME I GOT

PAID FOR IT...

WRITERS' TALES FROM THE

HOLLYWOOD TRENCHES

EDITED BY

PETER LEFCOURT & LAURA J. SHAPIRO

FOR

THE WRITERS GUILD FOUNDATION

WITH A FOREWORD BY **WILLIAM GOLDMAN**

PublicAffairs
New York

Published in the United States by PublicAffairs™, a member of the
Perseus Books Group.
All rights reserved.
Printed in the United States of America.

Book design and composition by Mark McGarry, Texas Type & Book Works.
Set in Minion

Library of Congress Cataloging-in-Publication Data
The first time I got paid for it . . . writers' tales from the Hollywood trenches / edited by
Peter Lefcourt & Laura J. Shapiro for the Writers Guild Foundation.—1st ed.
p. cm.
ISBN 1–58648–013–8
1. Motion picture authorship. 2. Screenwriters—United States—Biography.
I. Lefcourt, Peter II. Shapiro, Laura J. III. Writers Guild Foundation.
PN1996.F455 2000
812'.509—dc21
[B] 00–034151

FIRST EDITION
10 9 8 7 6 5 4 3 2 1

No man but a blockhead ever wrote, except for money.

SAMUEL JOHNSON

CONTENTS

PREFACE

THE FIRST TIME I heard of the Writers Guild Foundation* was in early 1997 when Laura Anne Edwards asked me to edit a commemorative book of essays by leading film and television writers for *Words Into Pictures,* a conference on the art and business of writing for the entertainment industry that she was executive producing. "I can't pay you very much," she said shamelessly, "but I'll make sure you meet everybody."

She was true to her word. In the last three years, through two *Words Into Pictures* commemorative books (1997 and 1999), and now this publication, I have had the good fortune to work with over seventy of the most talented, successful, and revered writers in the entertainment industry. They have all been enthusiastic,

*The Writers Guild Foundation, a nonprofit charitable corporation, is distinct from the Writers Guild of America, west, a union. (For more information, please see the note about the Foundation at the back of the book.)

generous, and helpful, donating their words and time (and royalties) to the Foundation.

In a business that all too often discounts the role of the writer, it is healing for us to read these stories. It gives us a sense of camaraderie that soothes the stress of facing the insanity of Hollywood and the wilderness of the blank page. It helps us to feel as if we were part of a community, and that is what this book, and the Writers Guild Foundation, represent. Through the process of editing these essays, I have found strength in the support and acceptance of these writers. It is my hope that while these pieces amuse and inform, they also offer some of that strength to the reader who aspires to write.

There are so many who must be thanked here: I wholeheartedly thank every one of the incredible writers in this book—your enthusiasm and participation have propelled this project beyond our wildest expectations. First and foremost among them, Peter Lefcourt, for making the published version of this book happen and for his generous support and editorial collaboration; Esther Newberg and ICM for representing the project; Geoff Shandler and everyone at PublicAffairs; Michael Donaldson for his tireless pro bono legal work and advocacy; the Foundation board of directors, especially those who helped us get writers to participate—our President, Tom Schulman, Vice President, Programs, Callie Khouri, and especially Vice President, Development, Allan Burns, for bringing in so many stellar contributors and for being such a paradigm of support and follow-through; the Foundation staff—Executive Director Pat Cummings, Program Director Angela Kirgo (who roped in a number of writers for the project), Librarian Karen Pedersen and her assistant Jimmy Bangley; a special thanks to all the assistants of the writers in this book for their help in prodding their employers about deadlines and paperwork; and finally, last but by no means least, Laura Anne Edwards for giving me the ball to run with in the first place.

LAURA J. SHAPIRO
EDITOR

FOREWORD BY WILLIAM GOLDMAN

THE FIRST TIME I ever had a catatonic fit was also the first time I ever sold a piece of writing. The two events are more than a little related.

This book is a bunch of memories from a bunch of storytellers about, little or big, moments when their lives took a leap, left a familiar orbit, landed somewhere strange. I've chosen one of my seminal moments, when the Fates did their dance, spun me around, altered everything. I think to at least try and understand my onetime catatonia, you have to know at least a little about what corner of the room I was coming from.

I was born in Chicago, 1931, and brought up in a then small commuter's town, Highland Park. The 8:08 was the morning train of choice; the 5:40 brought the fathers home.

Mine was a businessman's family. There were two children, my four-years-older brother, James, and myself. He went on to win an Oscar for writing *The Lion in Winter,* but in his teens, he wanted to be a music critic.

I had always wanted to be a writer, I don't know why. Probably because from earliest memory, I had loved story. I hid in books probably my first twenty years. I remember once picking up a play by O'Neill we had in our bookshelves, *Ah, Wilderness!*

I hated it so much I could not believe he was this genius playwright, so I went to the library and over that weekend, read everything he had ever written. Not such a big deal as I think back on it now. Except I was probably thirteen when I did it. So clearly, I read.

But my great love was comic books. I had many hundreds of them, all from what is now the golden age. My father was somehow on the mailing list for *Walt Disney's Comics and Stories.* He brought that home. And I would go to Larson's on Central with my allowance money for such wonders. The first Superman. Not just the first Batman but also the first Batman and Robin. Captain Marvel—and yes, I still know what SHAZAM stands for—the Sub Mariner, on and on.

If you are wondering what my collection is worth I will tell you this: zip. Because my mother, in an act of mother's evil bordering on Medea's, my mother, without asking or telling me, without so much as a fucking word, GAVE MY ENTIRE COLLECTION AWAY. To the soldiers at Fort Sheridan.

I don't remember writing these early years. Maybe I tried a one-page wonder when I was twelve or mid-teens. Doubt it, though. I just had this vague notion that being a writer would be neat, whatever that meant.

Then Irwin Shaw came along to save me.

I was eighteen and an aunt gave me a copy of *Mixed Company,* a book of his collected stories. I'd never read a word by him, never probably heard his name. But I remember the lead story in the book was "The Girls in Their Summer Dresses." About a guy who looked at women.

Followed by "The Eighty Yard Run." Now you probably all read this about me with all the millennium madness going on, so and so was the greatest this, such and such the greatest that.

Well, you must have seen the headlines proclaiming me "Sports Nut of the Century." In truth, the balloting wasn't even close.

Point being? Well, "The Eighty Yard Run" is about a football player. Shit, I remember thinking, can you do that? Can you write about stuff *I* care about? The *New Yorker,* by this time, had begun its endless publishing of bloodless stories about, say, an American couple, unhappily married, and they go to Europe maybe to change things and they end up in the Piazza San Marco where in the last paragraph a fly would walk across the table, and the story would always end like this: "And she understood."

I finished *Mixed Company* and probably didn't know the effect it would have on me. You see, Shaw wrote so easily. Never the wrong word. You just go happily along mostly unaware of the wonders happening around you.

Shaw is out of fashion today, which is too bad for you, because he is one of the great story writers in our history, and more than likely, you don't know that. He and F. Scott are my two guys, and I have zero doubts on that score.

So I would write like Irwin Shaw. (Easy money at the brick factory.) At eighteen, I began writing stories. Not a whole lot of instant acclaim. I took a creative writing course at Oberlin.

Everyone else took it because it was a gut course. I wanted a career. Everyone else got A's and B's, I got the only C.

I took a creative writing course at Northwestern one summer. Worst grade in the class. Oberlin had a literary magazine and I was the fiction editor. Two brilliant girls were involved with me. One was poetry editor, one the overall chief. Everything was submitted anonymously. Every issue I would stick a story of mine in the pile. And wait for their comments.

"Well, we can't publish this shit," they would say when my story came up for discussion. You understand: *I couldn't get a story of mine in a magazine when I was the fiction editor.*

I go in the Army after graduation, am sent to the Pentagon by mistake. Every evening I would go back to Fort Myers for dinner, then return to the Pentagon to write my stories.

And of course, send them out.

I have, somewhere, hundreds of rejection slips. Never a comment from an editor. Never anything but the fucking form note saying what I had written was not of interest at this time.

My confidence is not building through these years. I hope you get that.

Graduate school, Columbia. 1954–1956. My college grades are so bad I can't get accepted without pull, which was humiliating.

I kept sending out my stories. Kept getting the effing rejections. The suggestion is made I might return to Chicago after I got my master's and go into advertising. If I wanted to write, well, I could be a copywriter.

BUT I DIDN'T FUCKING WANT TO BE A COPYWRITER, DON'T YOU SEE?

June '56, and the end is near. I am done with college, done with the Army, done with grad school—I thought for a moment of getting a doctorate but then realized I would have to pass a number of language tests and I have no facility for languages. The ad agency was smiling at me evilly.

Where do you go when there's no place to go? You go home. So I went back to Highland Park where Minnie was. Tomine Barstad came to work for my family five years before I was born, left when I was in my forties, and more than anyone is the reason I'm alive today.

I would write and she could cook meals and sometimes I would take a break and we would have coffee in the kitchen. I had never written anything much longer than fifteen pages and pretty soon I was on page 50—and that was scary, I'd never been there before. And then page 75 and finally, three weeks after I started, on July 14th, page 187 and *The Temple of Gold* was finished.

I named it after the ending scene from *Gunga Din,* now and forever the greatest movie, where Sam Jaffe climbs up the temple of gold and saves the British troops and gets shot to death for it.

I held a novel in my hands. What a thing.

Query: what to do with it?

Cutting to the chase: A guy I knew in the Army knew an editor who hated dealing with agents so he became an agent so he could deal with writers. Joseph McCrindle. He read it, sent it to an editor he knew at Knopf. Who read it.

Now you are thinking the editor did one of two things—accepted it or turned it down.

Nope. He was kind of intrigued by what he'd read but he had no idea if I could write or not. So what he said was this: Double it in length and submit it again.

That still seems among the nuttier directives ever given to a first novelist. But after the standard days of panic, I did it. And submitted it again. And waited.

I was living in an apartment then with two others from the Midwest, my brother, who had now decided to become a playwright, and his oldest friend, John Kander from Kansas City, who wanted to be a composer someday but at that moment was stuck giving voice lessons. (Not forever though. He went on to write *Cabaret, Chicago, New York, New York,* etc., etc.)

And we had this sensational apartment. 344 West 72nd Street. nine rooms, and the front three had what is still, for me, *the* view of Manhattan—straight up the Hudson to forever. People now who are told the three of us, all young and feisty, were together trying to crack Magic Town find the thought romantic. I never felt it was anything but three nerds trying to get through the day.

The rent a total of 275 smackers. If you think that is amazing, know this: It had been on the market for six months at the gaudy number 300—and no one would take it. The rumor we were told was the previous tenants were six Juilliard piano students who went mad one night and had a piano-playing contest, all six banging away at the same time for hours till the management got them out. (Van Cliburn was reputed to be one of the six, but I never checked that out for fear that it might not turn out to be true. In my mind, now and forever, he was.)

I am alone in the apartment, wandering, hoping that somehow this all might actually happen. But no one, truly, truly, had any faith. A girl I was dating when I picked her up later that night gave me a present and when I asked what it was for she said it was something nice considering the publisher had rejected me.

And the phone rang—it must have—from now on I remember

almost nothing. And it was probably my agent saying that Knopf said yes.

I must have sounded pleased, but as I said, who knows. I just wandered around the apartment—Jim was up in Boston and John was out somewhere, so I walked around the place—it was railroad flat style so you could hike a far piece, as someone must have said.

When Kander came home he said have you heard and I must have told him they took it and he said probably, "Oh Billy, that's wonderful." And I must have allowed that it sure was.

Then he asked, Was everybody excited that I'd told? Hadn't told anybody, I answered.

By now he realized I was acting very weirdly indeed, so he saved me with these words: "Billy, would you like me to call people for you?"

How would we work that, I must have wondered.

"Well," Kander said, carefully, "what we could do is sit next to the phone and you could tell me who you wanted me to call and then I could call them and tell them the news and also that you were acting a little strange and didn't want to talk about it now."

I liked the sound of that so we did it. I remember sitting down next to him and he would say, "I think Sarah would be so happy for you, shall we call Sarah?" and I would nod and I can still hear him saying, "Sarah, Billy's book was taken by Knopf but he's not quite up to talking about it, would you like to say congratulations?" and then he would put the phone near me and Sarah would say, "it's just wonderful," and I would say "thank you, it is" and then John would tell her that I would call tomorrow and we went on down the line of all the people I knew.

I didn't know at the time that I was in a catatonic state, maybe a medico would say it was something else. But looking back on it, I'm satisfied that's what it was.

By the next day I was able to deal with the phone myself and life went on—but of course, it had changed, everything had changed.

I was a writer now. Later that week I went to a party and met a girl and she asked what I was doing in New York and I said I was a writer and she got this terrible look and said to me, "Oh, another one." And I was able to say I was, I really was, and Knopf was publishing my novel in the fall.

As I look back now, I guess the single most remarkable act of my decades of storytelling is that I somehow, in what desperation, what despair, what overall sense of failure and survival I know not, but somehow I wrote that book.

But I do know this: If Knopf says no, if all the publishers say that awful word, no, sorry, not for us, nothing we can use at this time, no, thanks but no—I never would have written again.

Which would not have greatly altered the course of Western culture a whole lot, and a number of people I know don't believe that I wouldn't have tried again.

But I do.

What I'm not totally sure of is why I went weird that day. I think the shock of suddenly being told I had talent after those early formative years of being told I had none, that had to be in there somewhere. So was the family fact that I wasn't supposed to succeed, my brother was.

Or maybe it's tied to an early and great Kander and Ebb song. A girl with no money and a lot of desperation has just gotten, amazingly, a job. This is what she sings:

When it all comes true
Just the way you planned
It's funny, but the bells don't ring,
It's a quiet thing...

Could be that. That movies have prepared us for The Big Deal, whistles tooting, but life doesn't work that way.

All I know is, it sure got awfully silent on West 72nd Street that wondrous day...

———

William Goldman has been writing books and movies for forty-five years. He has won three Lifetime Achievement Awards for Screenwriting, two Screenwriter of the Year Awards, two Academy Awards® (for *Butch Cassidy and the Sundance Kid* and *All the President's Men*), and one English Academy Award. His novels include *The Princess Bride* and *Marathon Man*, which has made him very famous in dentists' offices around the world.

7

THE FIRST TIME I GOT PAID FOR IT

ALAN ALDA

I was writing my first episode of *Mash* in a hotel room with French furniture from the Wilshire Boulevard period, and I noticed I had begun dancing around the room.

I was in the hotel because the architect who was doing renovations on our house had promised me the work would be finished by the time I came back to town for the second season of *Mash*, whose first season had paid for the house in the first place.

Renovations, like rewrites, take longer than expected, and I had made things worse by insisting that the house look like the plan we had agreed on before I left town. "I don't want that big excrescence in my living room," I had said, using the biggest word I could think of for a modernist hump on the wall the architect was proposing. Sure enough, when I got back to L.A., the house wasn't finished, but there was the hump, big as life, and just as excrescent. I took a sledgehammer to it and knocked it off the wall. This made my point, but set back construction another three weeks.

So, here I was, working on my first serious try at a television script in the cool, contemplative solitude that can only be found in a cheesy, fake-elegant hotel. More and more, I found myself taking a sledgehammer to my own scenes and dialogue, and after a while I was dancing.

I was dancing because, after hours of rewriting a scene, I had finally solved it and had crashed through to something I knew would work. "I can do it . . . ! I can do it!" I chanted, dancing and jumping for joy until the thought intruded that there were another few dozen problems to solve before I'd be finished.

This was the first time since I had decided I wanted to be a writer at the age of eight that I was actually working on something that might be seen by millions of people. Every little writing victory was therefore charged with emotion.

I've thought, since then, how lucky I was that my first script was one in which so many problems had already been solved for me. The show had been on the air for a year: I wasn't creating characters from scratch; I wasn't imagining a whole new world.

As an actor, I had already researched the time and place. I'd read that the Korean winters were bitter and, in a series of two-handed scenes, I let a humble pair of longjohns go from one shivering body to another through a string of deals, love offerings and extortions. It was, of course, similar to a device used by Schnitzler in the film *La Ronde,* so even some of the plot was borrowed.

In this way, I was able to concentrate on the pleasures of putting words together, discovering the voices of the characters, tracking the subsurface tectonics of their emotions. This made my victory dances a whole lot easier to come by than I realized at the time. Even after I had written a number of episodes and was exploring new paths, I was still making use of the work of people who had first explored the territory.

It was something of a shock when I began working on the first feature-length script I'd try after writing for *Mash*. Since it would be three times longer than an episode, I assumed it would be about three times harder. Imagine my surprise when it turned out to be about 27 times harder.

Suddenly, I had to create, through research and imagination, a new world, populated by characters I had to build from their heads to their toes. I had to find out how they would act on one another in a way that would plunge them into Act Two and let them climb out through Act Three. I was all by myself on a huge construction site.

Hemingway said that writing is architecture, not interior decoration. I was learning that, even with all the rewriting, it wasn't renovations, either.

Now I was taking a sledgehammer to the foundation itself, re-designing it time after time, from scratch.

After all that, when I would finally crash through to something that worked, I would feel—and every writer must feel something like this—a thrill, a rush of joy, a desire to dance around the room.

I still feel it. And, once in a while, I still dance.

———

Alan Alda has written five screenplays: *The Seduction of Joe Tynan, Four Seasons, Sweet Liberty, A New Life,* and *Betsy's Wedding.* He wrote eighteen episodes of *Mash,* one of which, *Inga,* won him an Emmy for writing.

TINA ANDREWS

THE FIRST TIME I took a meeting as a professional screenwriter was on a proposed project for PBS called *Alex Haley's Great Men of African Descent*. Unbeknownst to me, Alex had been forwarded a spec script I'd written two years earlier called *The Mistress of Monticello,* which chronicled Sally Hemings's troubled yet devoted relationship with Thomas Jefferson, and he was impressed. So one day I'm sitting at home wondering how I was going to pay either the phone bill or the rent, and the phone rang. "Great," I'm thinking. "At least the phone's still working." Lo and behold a somewhat familiar voice was on the other end. "Is this Tina Andrews?" "Yes," I answered tentatively, after all it could have been a bill collector (my Visa payment was in arrears too). The voice continued, "Is this the same Tina Andrews who was in *Roots*?" Now my curiosity was piqued. "Yes," I answered more definitively. Someone referencing *Roots* didn't want cash. "Well, this is Alex Haley."

I nearly died. I hadn't seen Alex since I'd taken part as an actress in the most respected, most revered miniseries of all time. Now suddenly I, who can be very verbal, was struck dumb. Words failed me, my voice mute forcing Alex to echo "Are you there?" When I finally picked myself off the floor and found my voice all I could repeat was "Oh my God!" Eventually I calmed down enough for us to have an intelligent conversation—even though the bulk of my end was a few "uh huh's" and "I agrees." He then told me he'd requested other of my writing samples from my agency and complimented me on the Hemings project and my piece on Bob Marley. He felt I had a good grasp on scripting biographies and wondered if I could fly down to his farm in Kentucky to meet with him, perhaps stay a few days and brainstorm the PBS project. Again, I nearly fainted. Brainstorm with Alex Haley?

Suddenly, I became nervous. I'd be spending several days with a literary genius. A wordsmith whose novel sat down every man, woman, and child in this country for eight nights straight and forced them to examine America and the ills of slavery and racism through the resilience of his indomitable family. It changed the face of television. And here he was doing another television series on the lives of great Black men and women whose stories needed to be told. And he wanted *me* to brainstorm with him?

Well obviously I got over my trepidations and found myself on a plane bound for Kentucky. Alex and his assistant, Gertie, met me at the airport. We hugged and caught up on all the actors who were in *Roots* while Alex showed me the countryside. When we reached his farm he showed me to one of eight houses on the compound which would be mine for my four-day stay. It was

called the "duck house" as everything in it was feminine and decorated with all things duck—photos, pillows, whatnots, even
chairs carved into ducks. I settled in. That night over fresh-
caught trout Alex and I discussed the project. How we'd approach it. Who we'd chronicle first. During this discussion I saw
an unusual art object on a wall. A nickel, a dime, and three pen-
nies were backed against black velvet and ensconced in a
Plexiglas container. When I asked Alex about this, he smiled and
declared it was what he had in his pocket the day he discovered
Roots was being published. 18 cents! He further explained he'd
only had wilting lettuce, two catsup packets, and a half-empty jar
of Miracle Whip in his refrigerator. His plan was to have a salad
with french dressing for dinner that very night. Suddenly, I didn't
feel bad about my mounting bills for I had far more than 18
cents. I had a mentor—a great Sage.

We went to work the next day. Alex hated computers and
used his time-honored old typewriter. We sat side by side—me
with my laptop, Alex clicking away on his upright Royal. Gertie
prepared our meals. On our breaks we'd walk the acreage of
Haley farm finding artifacts, interesting rocks and unusual
plants. He even found an ancient Indian arrowhead which he
gave me. He encouraged me to keep exploring the controversial.
Not to be afraid of criticism. To be an "artist," which meant being
true to one's art. He insisted I not let my enthusiasm for my Sally
Hemings project die just because I couldn't get it produced.
"Keep working on it. Keep improving it. Keep slugging." I could
listen to him all night. And by the end of the fourth day, we were
well on our way with the pilot for the PBS project which chronicled my suggestion—Alexandre Dumas.

I flew back to Los Angeles with the Indian arrowhead in my pocket for good luck and Alex's spirit in my heart. I wrote vigilantly. Almost as though Alex himself was just over my shoulder saying, "Write from the heart. Don't be afraid." I was in touch with Alex once a week for the next two months. He was interested in my developing his project on Madame C. J. Walker. However, he had so many speaking engagements we would not be able to discuss the project for a month. But he promised to have a get-together at his farm around the time of my birthday in April so I could meet two of his friends who are my heroes— Maya Angelou and Oprah Winfrey.

It was not to be. Nor was the PBS project.

I arose one morning two weeks later to the news Alex Haley had died, of diabetes and, I suspect, his work schedule, of which I'd warned him. What a tragedy! Sixty-five years old with so much left to give the world. I could not face my computer for weeks . . . until his voice echoed in my ear one day, "Tina, it's time to write!"

These days I think about Alex Haley a lot. About his legacy—and his effect on my life in particular. As a result of our PBS project I was given story points toward admittance to the WGA. Having worked with him as a writer gave me a certain cachet, which two months after his death led to my first screenplay assignment at Columbia Pictures and a career boost. At least these days I can pay my phone bill. And the Sally Hemings project? It was produced as a four-hour miniseries for CBS in February of 2000 and became the highest-rated, most watched miniseries of February sweeps. Alex's spirit is still with me. His voice still whispering in my ear, "Write from the heart. Don't be afraid." His lessons guiding me through the maze of stories from the African American experience which still need to be told. And I hear him. Thanks, Alex.

––––––––––

Tina Andrews is the screenwriter and co-executive producer of the upcoming CBS miniseries *Jacqueline Bouvier Kennedy Onassis,* and the four-hour CBS miniseries, *Sally Hemings: An American Scandal,* which aired in February 2000; she was also the screenwriter for the 1998 Warner Bros. release *Why Do Fools Fall in Love?* and was named one of "50 to Watch" by *Daily Variety.*

STEVEN BOCHCO

THE FIRST TIME I ever got a "Written by" credit was in 1967. I was a naive, twenty-three-year-old kid one year out of college, a wanna-be writer working at Universal Studios, and I was told to meet with a cigar-chomping veteran producer on the lot named Harry Tatelman, who somehow managed to mangle my name sufficiently so that every time he addressed me as "Steve," it always came out—muffled by that cheap stogie jammed between his tobacco-stained teeth—sounding like "Stiff." Based on what I was about to agree to, I suppose it was an apt moniker.

Harry was in charge of expanding unsold one-hour pilots and anthological dramas into two-hour movies, which Universal would then package and sell to overseas markets. I was assigned to stretch an original one-hour television drama entitled *A Slow Fade to Black,* which had aired on NBC's Chrysler Theater, a successful anthology series then being produced by Universal. I'd graduated from Carnegie Tech (now Carnegie-Mellon) one year earlier as a playwriting major, and knew virtually nothing about writing for film. But under Harry's and the director's guidance, I blithely commenced expansion of the original script, with specific instructions not to write any scenes which included the original cast of characters, because the actors (including Rod Steiger and Robert Culp) were too expensive.

A Slow Fade to Black was about a hugely successful, hard-nosed, first-generation American who'd made it big as one of the original Hollywood movie moguls (think Harry Cohen). Since I couldn't write any added scenes using the existing characters, my only viable alternative was to write an hour's worth of flashbacks, dramatizing the early lives of the characters—their dreams, their struggles, and the early failures and successes which preceded their rise to Hollywood fame and fortune. In so doing, I had to deconstruct the original script, figure out where the flashback scenes were supposed to go, and then reassemble the new, two-hour movie version. It was a frightening task for a young, inexperienced writer and, in retrospect, I thank God for the supervision of the producer and director, without whose guidance and encouragement I would have been totally lost. Of course, also in retrospect, it was a dreadful (not to mention destructive) piece of work, and if there's a Writer's Heaven, and the original author of *A Slow Fade to Black* is on the Admissions Committee, I am probably doomed to eternity in Writer's Hell.

In any event, I completed the shooting script, Harry and his director (a wonderful old guy named Joe Leytes) cast young look-a-likes of the middle-aged stars, and I watched in amazement as the first words I'd ever written for the screen were filmed. During the entire project, lasting several months from beginning to end, I never once met with or consulted the original writer of the fine drama I was butchering, and as a first-time screenwriter, not yet even a member of the Writers Guild, I had no idea that I'd even receive a screen credit. So when I was invited to a showing of the finished product, and for the first time saw my name on the screen sharing credit with the original writer, I was simultaneously thrilled and embarrassed, because the writer whose sole credit I'd now taken partial custody of was none other than the famed Rod Serling.

———

Award-winning television writer/producer **Steven Bochco** has co-created numerous ground-breaking series including *Hill Street Blues, L.A. Law, Doogie Howser M.D., Cop Rock, Civil Wars, Murder One,* and *NYPD Blue.*

ERIC BOGOSIAN

BLOODIED BUT UNBOWED

THE FIRST TIME I got paid to write was in 1986 when a solo theater piece I had been doing, *Drinking in America,* had been selling out at the American Place Theater in New York. The studios were "buying" like crazy. Scott Rudin, the reigning wunderkind studio head at Fox, had a penchant for the theatrical. So I got six figures to write a comedy in which I would star. Kind of an Armenian Eddie Murphy kind of thing, dig? I had never written a screenplay. Why not learn on the job?

Some backstory here. Prior to 1986 I existed pretty much outside of any kind of show-biz loop. For years I had worked "downtown," writing and performing in places like The Kitchen or The Mudd Club or Club 57. I was having the time of my life, but 1984 found me strung out and broke. Unless I was planning to exchange my rat-infested storefront on Elizabeth Street for a cardboard box on the Bowery, the life I was leading was not viable.

So when the solo took off, I welcomed a new lifestyle in which I could buy fresh vegetables, paper towels, and other luxuries with impunity. Every week I got a fat paycheck from American Place. Casting people wanted to see me. Cinemax was going to shoot the show. The phone was ringing, calls from the West Coast. *Rolling Stone* and *People* did profiles. Yada. Yada. Yada. And now the crowning achievement, a "deal" at a "major." I was going to be a player, I was going to take meetings.

My wife, Jo Bonney, and I bought a house in New Jersey so we could live and breathe like humans. I bought new clothes. Jo became pregnant. My agent started returning my phone calls, even took me out to lunch. I bought a new Apple IIe computer. I bought an oak rolltop desk, to sit at while I wrote my screenplay.

I bought a Syd Field book. I learned what a plot point was. I was going to figure out how to write. Instead, I learned my first lessons about how movies don't get made in L.A. (I want to note here that I'm not bitter or anything like that. I had fun. Just a different kind of fun than I had expected.)

In hindsight, of course, I thought I would write a screenplay, everyone would fall in love with it, and in a few months it would get cast and shot. This would be followed by more screenplay work, and eventually offers to direct. I'd become rich and important. I'd be driven around in a stretch limo. I would revolutionize cinema.

You could say I was a dreamer. You could say I was a fool.

Anyway, I hacked away at a draft for a few months. There were some very nice people here in New York whose job it was to oversee my "pages." I'm sure my stuff sucked out loud. Like most writers who start out in another medium, I wrote my filmscript with no sense of film construction. My pages featured lots of cars

driving up and down dark streets, flashbacks, voice-over narra-
tion. My dialogue went on for pages. Lots of characters, in fact I
introduced a new character in almost every scene.

No story line. No imagery. Just lots of pages. I would count
the pages to see how well I was doing. I would call my agent and
tell him how many pages I had written that day. I figured when I
had enough pages, I'd be finished. He humored me.

Fall arrived. My wife was starting to show the pregnancy. We
shot the Cinemax special. I owed Joe Papp a play in which I
would star. I was supposed to start rehearsals in March. I wanted
to get the first draft of the screenplay done so we could start pre-
production already! Not to mention, I needed the money for delivery of first draft to pay off all my new expenses.

I sent in my draft and got shipped out to L.A. Fox put me up
in the Beverly Wilshire Hotel. I was very impressed with how
fancy it was. The room didn't have wallpaper, it had padded cloth
walls. A driver took me over to "the lot" and I met with Sara
Colleton, a tall cool beauty, the Fox executive in charge of my
project. I think she was wearing jodhpurs. There was a riding
crop propped against the wall behind her desk.

Sara gushed about how wonderful my draft was. Really excellent. Then she said "we" would like to suggest a few changes. She
was the only person from the studio there. I assumed by "we" she
meant she and Scott. Hah! She said, let's turn to page one. Two
hours later she had thrown out every page of the draft.

As I stumbled out of the office, my entire life in disarray, Sara
made the wry remark: "His head is bloodied, but unbowed." I
couldn't breathe. The driver dropped me back to my room. I had
an anxiety attack. Now the padded walls of my room made sense.

From my New York producers, I heard the words, "Well, you

could pass this in, but the important thing is to get a script that is makeable. That's what we all want. Why don't you give it another pass?" It wouldn't be the last time I heard words like these from a producer.

Two months later I sent in the finished script. It went into immediate turnaround. What I hadn't realized was that by the time my deal had been completed and I had started writing, the project was already dead in the water. Scott was off to greener pastures, I was no longer flavor of the month. But I had a job to do, so I did it. And I got paid.

———

Eric Bogosian is the author of three plays, *Talk Radio, subUrbia,* and *Griller* as well as six solo shows, including the Obie Award—winning *Sex, Drugs, Rock & Roll* and *Pounding Nails in the Floor with My Forehead.* As a screenwriter he has worked for Paramount, 20th Century-Fox, Warner Bros., New Line, Sam Goldwyn, Universal, HBO, Lumiere, and Castle Rock. He adapted both *Talk Radio* and *subUrbia* for film. His new solo, *Wake Up and Smell the Coffee,* opened in New York in the spring of 2000.

ALLAN BURNS

GODS & MUNSTERS

ACTUALLY I had been paid for it before, a princely $217 a week writing for *Rocky and Bullwinkle* at Jay Ward's tumble-down little cartoon factory directly across Sunset Boulevard from the Chateau Marmont. My first partner and I, sensing that our budding comedy gifts might extend beyond writing dialogue for goofy animals and that we were not likely to be tanning in Tahiti on a measly eight hundred-plus a month, sought out an agent we'd heard of at the old Ashley-Steiner Agency. Let's call him Lester, since that was his name. Lester, after hearing some of our pitches for comedy series, agreed to take us on as clients on a contingency basis, which is to say the moment we left his office we dropped off his radar screen. When, after a few weeks, we'd tried to contact him at the agency, we were brusquely informed that "Mister _____ is no longer employed by Ashley-Steiner," and when we pressed for details as to his current whereabouts, found ourselves talking to a dial tone. When Lester eventually did resurface, it was to inform us that he'd taken a job as head of television comedy development at a large studio, let's call it Universal, and, remembering one of our pitches that had to do with a family of bizarros that we had cleverly named *The Munsters,* invited us to meet and discuss developing our idea into a pilot script. We were, of course, thrilled. (Had we known that Lester had found his new job at Universal after being told of it by a veteran comedy writer client who'd asked Lester to try to get the job for *him,* we might have been a tad less thrilled at the prospect of getting involved with him. But we didn't know that. Yet.) And had we been less naive we might have found it faintly suspicious that we never met with Lester at the studio, only over breakfast (going dutch, perhaps another hint of what was to come) in cheap coffee shops, where we discussed the development of a story line for our script (Lester's contributions being limited to adenoidal snorts punctuated by dark frowns and thoughtful lip-pursing) and occasionally handed him pages that he stuffed into his coat pockets. We turned in the script, never thinking to be crass enough to press for payment, didn't hear a word from him, negative or positive, and in the ensuing months signed with an agent who had a nice office over the old Scandia restaurant kitchen that always smelled pungently of *gravlax* and *frikkedellar.* Unlike Lester, whose Cro-Magnon appearance would have landed him a role in *Two Million B.C.* without a lick of makeup, our new representative, Peter, was a patrician-looking, dapper fellow, well dressed, well read and well spoken, who drove a vintage Bentley—but whose rabid John Birch Society leanings, we'd soon learn, had gotten him summarily barred from the offices of most of the liberal comedy producers to whom we were so desperate to pitch. Nevertheless, we busied ourselves with developing other projects and pretty much forgot about Lester and our Munster script. Then one day Peter called, very jovial. "Did you see the trades today?" he asked. We hadn't. "*The Munsters* pilot is a go. In fact, it goes into production tomorrow. The director is a buddy of mine. I'll pick you up and we'll go out there."

Here's how dumb we were. (And how dumb he was, come to think of it. The Birch Society thing must have already begun to eat away at his brain.) Why did none of us find it particularly suspicious that, after six months of absolutely no communication from anyone at the studio regarding our script, here it was, suddenly in production? But off we went, in Peter's brown-over-tan Bentley with its buttery leather armchair seats, across Laurel Canyon to Universal and a soundstage a-bustle with first-day excitement, not the least of which ours as we looked around in awe at witnessing our idea turned into reality. Terrific set, very spooky and atmospheric, like we'd pictured. But our main characters, described in our script as simply bizarre-looking, had been transmogrified into Frankenstein's monster, Count Dracula and his daughter. We were taken somewhat aback, but no more than in the next moment, when Peter herded us over to the director, who was peering through the viewfinder of the camera. "Hey, Norman," he said, as the director turned and scowled at him for bothering him in the middle of lining up his shot, "I want you to meet the guys who wrote this." Norman shook his head. "No, they didn't. Norm and Ed did," he said. And turned back to the viewfinder.

In fact, we met Norm and Ed moments later. Nice fellows. Contract writers at the studio. Who *had* in fact written the script. And who'd had no inkling that the series idea Lester had pitched to them was actually the brainchild of a couple of cartoon writers whose brains he'd been picking over (dutch) breakfast meetings. Norm and Ed, to their credit, were as nonplussed as we. Soon Lester scurried up, working the set, doing his first-day-of-production glad handing. The amazing thing is he didn't seem the least bit fazed when he found himself face-to-face with Norm and Ed—and my partner and me. In fact, he appeared to only vaguely recognize us. But we were, after all, almost six months older than the last time he'd seen us.

Unlike many Hollywood horror stories, this one has a happy ending. It has to do with the Writers Guild of America and its then executive director, the famously feisty Michael Franklin. Since we weren't Guild members (animation writers not being covered by our union; sad to say, they still aren't), we went hat in hand to the old headquarters on Beverly Boulevard to inform Mike of what had transpired. Could he do anything for us, we wondered? A crooked little smile crossed his lips. His eyes twinkled. "Let me get into this," he said, his pink little tongue flicking involuntarily.

The money Mike and the Guild squeezed out of the studio bought me and my wife our first modest house.

My partner and I never had the opportunity to write a *Munsters* episode. We didn't "understand the concept." Or so the producers informed our agent.

The addition my wife and I put onto our house the next year we always thought of as "Lester's Room."

———

Allan Burns learned from this experience, went on to get a liberal agent and win six Emmys for such shows as *He & She, Mary Tyler Moore, Rhoda,* and *Lou Grant,* and receive an Oscar nomination for *A Little Romance.* He lives in an even nicer house, but has still never vacationed in Tahiti.

PETER CASEY

THE FIRST TIME my partners and I pitched our series idea for *Frasier* to NBC was, by far, the most memorable and bizarre network meeting I have been a part of in over twenty years as a television writer.

As any writer who has ever toiled in trenches of television will tell you, a pitch meeting with the network is never eagerly anticipated. From the moment it is set on the calendar it is viewed with suspicion, trepidation, and a general air of queasiness. There is a simple reason for all this apprehension. Your idea, your golden child, your painstakingly crafted premise and characters, will be twisted, stretched, bent and generally worked over like some luckless gambler who's delinquent on his debt. If you're lucky, you'll walk out of the network with a show that resembles the one with which you walked in. If you're unlucky, your idea will be rejected and you'll walk out empty-handed. If you're really unlucky you'll walk away with a revamped "network" version of your idea that you hate and an on-the-air commitment for thirteen.

My partners, David Lee and David Angell, and I had a long-term relationship with NBC. We had written and produced *Cheers* for them. When we formed our own company, Grub Street Productions, our first project, *Wings,* went to the peacock network. We were on very good terms with them and we knew they desperately needed this new series built around the *Cheers* character of Frasier Crane to succeed since *Cheers* was about to end its eleven-year run. One would think all these elements would add up to a cakewalk for us at the network. However, NBC's need for this to be a hit made us uneasy. What lengths were they willing to go to for this project to succeed? Kelsey Grammer and Pamela Sue Anderson? Frasier moves in across the hall from three sexy, scantily clad aerobics instructors? Couple these concerns with the dreadful track record of spin-offs and the certainty that our project would be constantly compared to its classic predecessor, and it's understandable why, in February of 1993, we were ushered into Warren Littlefield's office not quite knowing what to expect.

Joining Warren for the meeting were two NBC vice presidents, Perry Simon and Jamie Tarses. After the obligatory small talk they asked to hear our idea. It should be noted that for years Grub Street had told NBC in no uncertain terms that it would never, under any circumstances, do a family sitcom. We didn't do "cute." No kids. No dogs. Forget it. So we knew it would come as a bit of a shock to our hosts when David Lee started the pitch by saying,

"From the people who swore they would never do a family comedy . . ."

Still, none of us were prepared for what happened the moment those words were uttered. Perry Simon fell off the couch onto the floor. Hello? Perry Simon? NBC vice president? A rumpled pile of Armani on the floor? There was a moment of stunned silence, then good-natured laughter as Perry climbed back onto the couch. Usually the first network interruption is an annoying note. This was a good start.

My partners and I proceeded to take turns explaining in detail how Frasier was now divorced from Lilith, how he had returned to his hometown of Seattle, and how he'd begun a new career as a radio talk-show host. All through this part of the pitch something very strange was happening. Something that had never happened in a meeting like this before. They listened. Bless their hearts, they simply listened and let us tell it the way we envisioned it. It was truly weird . . . and wonderful. We forged ahead fearful that any pause would be filled with an avalanche of notes.

It was now time to pitch the first of the new supporting characters. When creating a character on paper it is often helpful to picture a certain actor playing the part. Usually by the time you finish creating your premise you have a "dream cast" in your head. It is common practice when pitching to the network to use your "dream cast" to give the executives a better handle on the characters. Nobody expects you to actually get your "dream cast." It's just a point of reference.

We began to describe Niles by saying, "Picture David Hyde Pierce."

When we finished our character description of Niles, Warren Littlefield said, "If you can get David Hyde Pierce, he's preapproved."

The weirdness was continuing. By telling us we needn't look

any further than David Hyde Pierce, Warren had simplified our jobs tremendously.

Casting for a pilot is, at best, migraine-inducing. You are forced to hear your carefully crafted jokes read over and over again by dozens of actors, some good, some not. You begin to loathe the lines you were so unabashedly proud of only weeks before. You get short-tempered with everyone. You find yourself absentmindedly envying that kid in the drive-thru window at McDonald's for the simplicity of his existence. And when you finally find two or three actors you're happy with for the part, you have to take them to read for the network. If the network doesn't approve any of them, the whole mind-numbing process begins all over again. Hence, our jubilation with David's preapproval.

The next character we pitched was Frasier's father, Martin.

"Picture John Mahoney," we said.

"If you can get John Mahoney, he's preapproved," said Warren.

My partners and I exchanged sideways glances. We would have loved to go for the trifecta. Unfortunately, our "dream cast" actor to play the part of Martin's home health care worker was Rosie Perez and she was a movie star. We knew there was no chance of getting her. However, we had mentioned that this character could be either Hispanic or English, so Warren said,

"If you make her English, you should check out Jane Leeves. We love Jane Leeves."

We loved the suggestion. Since we had already broken our unbreakable rule about doing a family comedy there was no reason to hold anything back. We told them about Eddie, the dog. At that moment, it could not have gotten any warmer or fuzzier in that executive office. It was as if every lucky star in the cosmos had fallen into perfect alignment.

When we finally concluded our pitch, Warren, Perry, and Jamie looked at each other and nodded. Then Warren said,

"We love it. Go do it."

We sat there for a moment, not sure if we had heard correctly. Privately, I was going through inner turmoil. On one hand, I wanted to casually stroll out of Warren's office as if what had just transpired was perfectly normal. Then, when the door closed behind me, make a mad dash to my car and race out of Burbank before they started tinkering with our idea. On the other hand, I had a very simple, yet potentially dangerous, question. If I asked it and got the wrong answer I would be dog meat with my partners. A wiser man would have kept his mouth shut. Wisdom was never my strong suit. I cleared my throat.

"No notes?" I asked.

I could feel the heat of my partners' stares on either side of me. If I could have, I would have snatched those words out of the air and shoved them back in my mouth. My partners were considering shoving something else in my mouth. Something that would hurt. A lot.

Warren looked over at Perry and Jamie. They shook their heads.

"No notes," said Warren.

In the world of network pitch meetings this was hitting one on the screws three hundred yards down the middle of the fairway. It was throwing a perfect game. It was winning the Super Bowl. Never before in my experience, and never since, has any network meeting approached the exquisite sublimity of that February afternoon. We had captured lightning in a bottle.

Still, I shudder to think what my partners would have done to me if Warren had answered that question differently.

Peter Casey is the co-creator and executive producer of *Frasier*. His career in television started in 1979 as a writer for *The Jeffersons*. In 1985, he began a three-and-a-half-year tenure as a writer/producer for *Cheers*. In 1989, along with his partners, David Lee and David Angell, he formed Grub Street Productions. The first show they created was the popular comedy, *Wings;* their second show was the highly acclaimed *Frasier*.

Peter is a twelve-time Emmy nominee and a seven-time Emmy winner. In 1995, he and his partners were named Television Producers of the Year by the Producers Guild of America. He has also received the Golden Globe, the People's Choice Award, the Humanitas Prize, and the George Foster Peabody Award.

T. S. COOK

THE FIRST TIME ... I ever walked on a set where a script of mine was being shot I developed a sudden case of leprosy. Or so it seemed.

This was in 1977 and the show was an episode of *Baretta* being shot on a stage at Universal. This was my "break" and I was excited, to say the least. I had savored the genteel poverty of a Hollywood newcomer for two years, watching TV series, learning the rhythms of several shows, and then writing the obligatory spec episodes. I had dozens of 'em. Indeed, the most frustrating day of my life (up 'til then; I've had worse since) was the afternoon I learned that the producer of *Gunsmoke* loved my spec, only to read that night in the trades that the show had been canceled. After only a century or two on the air. Impeccable timing, mine. That night, I got drunk and stabbed a clothes drier with a Bowie knife. I didn't like the way it was looking at me.

So, on that bright morning in '77, waltzing onto the sound stage to hear my dialogue immortalized, I was light-headed with pride. When I arrived, the stage was dark and everyone seemed to be on break. I saw the story editor and the executive producer across the expanse of the floor and waved to them. They turned their backs. I saw the director huddled with some camera crew guys and started toward him, but he beat a hasty retreat out into the daylight. Even the craft-service guy handed me my coffee and then dived for his foxhole. What was this? I had gone from being a fair-haired "young writer find" to having a face Father Damien couldn't love. Usually this transition takes at least half a season. What had I done wrong?

Slowly, I became aware of the source of this black mood, the event horizon of that morning: Series star Robert Blake was sitting all alone in a highboy chair in the middle of the sound stage. Blake was a notoriously difficult actor. He had crafted his psychotic persona over many visits to the *Tonight Show,* then starring Johnny Carson. Funny for the folks at home before lights out, treacherous for those who worked with him on a daily basis. I had been warned about "Bobby."

But that morning, leprosy or not, I was Superman. What could be so bad? There he was, all alone, reading what was obviously my script and deeply absorbed in it. If no one was going to come forward to introduce me to the star, I, author, would advance across the stage floor and stick out my hand. I hadn't gotten this far by being shy.

I was about halfway there when Blake leaped from the chair in a single, explosive move, hurled the script to the floor and cried for the world to hear: *"Who writes this shit?!"*

Curly of the Three Stooges used to do a wild, speedy one-eighty

when he spied trouble ahead, burbling "Whub-bub-bub-bub-bub
..." as he went. He could have taken lessons from me that morning. I was safely back in the shadows behind craft service before
"shit?!" echoed.

Some minutes later, the "Blakasaurus" retreated to its graffiti-
covered trailer and those smaller creatures who survive by stealth
made their way out into the light. The producer, executive producer and story editor were all hiding out that morning, which
indicated just how torrential the storm had been. Now they were
being summoned to a "story conference" in the trailer. They
asked me to come along. Actually, the phrase they used was "join
the staff for a story conference." As we all know, joining the staff
is the brass ring, so I tagged along.

The exterior walls of the trailer radiated heat. The interior
was a lava tube. "Bobby" looked me up and down and said I
could stay. "Listen, kid," he told me. (Ah, the days when I could
still be called "kid.") "You've got a good ear for the street, but
you've got to learn what the people in Iowa want and give it to
them." Now, I was perfectly willing to concede that Robert Blake
had spent more time on "the street" than I. But this "kid" had
lived two and a half years in Iowa, had loved it and knew it well. I
was contemplating whether I should point this out to him when
he handed me a copy of the script they had been shooting that
morning and proceeded to parse a scene with me. I took one
look at the scene and realized that I had not written a word of
this. Sometime in the long nights preceding production someone had done a "polish."

As I listened to Blake's scathing critique of "my" scene structure, I wondered what to do. Leap up and tell the truth? Claim
innocence and join him in artistic outrage? That would be the

feel-good thing to do. Yet as I looked around cautiously at the others in the trailer, none of whom was saying a thing, I discovered a gift I didn't know I had: I could divine who had written these lines. There were clues only another writer could see—the masked discomfort and sublimated peeve of a talented man, whose post-midnight attempts to balance budget, schedule and art were being publicly ridiculed by an actor who never had to worry about such things.

I liked the story editor. He'd been very helpful to me in my revisions of the episode and I wanted to work with him, with all of them, again. So I shut my mouth and absorbed Blake's misdirected tirade. To tell the truth, it didn't hurt as much as I thought it would.

These days, some twenty years later, I don't absorb tirades as well or as willingly as I used to. Nor do I have to—for the most part my relationships with my fellow artists have been warm and collegial. I guess if there's a point to this story, it is that we writers should always be sensitive to the pride and emotional needs of our fellows.

And we should all know how to do the Curly One-Eighty.

T. S. Cook is an Emmy- and Oscar-nominated writer specializing in drama taken from real life. Credits include *The China Syndrome* for the big screen, *Scared Straight, The Switch,* and *Texas Justice* for network TV, and *Nightbreaker* for cable TV. He is currently writing *Making Monsters* for HBO, a modern-day Frankenstein story set within the mind-maze of contemporary psychiatry.

Tom believes that well-crafted, emotionally involving drama can help people determine how they feel about personal and social issues. And that it has ever been so. Journalism has a wonderful transitory value, but, as he is fond of saying, "In what did Shakespeare wrap his fish?"

CAMERON CROWE

LEAVE 'EM LAUGHING

THE YEAR was 1982, and this was the afternoon I would see a rough-cut screening of the first film I had written, *Fast Times at Ridgemont High*. Already it was a gloomy day, legendarily bad. John Belushi had died the night before, and we stood on the lot of the studio whose films had turned him into a sensation. A few of the film company executives, along with friends and family, filed into the theater to view our movie. The worst kind of depression filled the air.

We watched a jumpy black-and-white copy of the film. The movie looked ragged, and it played even worse. Only a few embarrassed laughs cut the silence. Every few minutes I leaned over and whispered urgently into my girlfriend's ear. "I'm dying," I said. "I'm dead." The movie was shuffled off to the dregs of summer, released in far fewer theaters than the studio had originally discussed. There were no champagne-filled, self-congratulatory limousine rides across the city on that opening Friday night. No cruising of the theaters to check the lines. The studio itself seemed to be in denial that it was even releasing it at all. Its hopes were pinned to the film that had occupied all the bigger stages and all its dreams of a huge cash windfall, *The Best Little Whorehouse in Texas*.

I was in denial too. I took off on Saturday morning with a buddy, and we drove to the Arizona wedding of a fellow journalist. Somewhere past the California state line, curiosity got the better of me. I persuaded my buddy to cruise some rural Arizona theaters to see how we were doing. We were shocked to find a full lobby of moviegoers in a theater showing *Fast Times*. Convinced it was an aberration, we drove a little farther and checked a theater in Tucson. Another packed house. We got out of the car and sneaked into the lobby. I'll never forget the kid standing near the popcorn line, already wearing checkerboard tennis shoes like Jeff Spicoli (Sean Penn) wore in the movie. "I know that dude!" he kept saying, cracking up his friends. It all felt like someone's cruel and elaborate practical joke.

Quietly, I stood at the back of the theater and listened to the oddest thing—waves of laughter at lines I had written. And the biggest laughs were coming from the smallest moments. Quiet looks. The terrible behavior of The Rat (Brian Backer), faced with a brazen advance from Stacy (Jennifer Jason Leigh), the girl he was infatuated with. The simple act of Spicoli entering All-American Burger like a stoned emperor. The audience was already hooting and applauding him and he hadn't said a word.

It is the most delicate, surprising and indefinable thing—what makes an audience laugh—but I knew I was hooked. I had expected to attend the wedding as a failure, instead I arrived with a lifelong job. I tried to say it as often and as coolly as I could. "Me? I'm a screenwriter."

There are no lasting formulas to comedy, but I've found a few theories over the years. Comedy is like bass fishing. Everyone is an expert, the fish is smarter than all of them, and the flashiest, shiniest lures never work. Always, the audience will make its own discoveries. The mere whiff of someone working overtime, straining for a laugh, is the biggest laugh killer of all.

With a tip of the hat to manic geniuses like the Marx Brothers and Jim Carrey, who manage to make their intricate and bizarre humor look spontaneous, the great moments of comedy tend to be stolen moments. The joke you never expected. Director Ernst Lubitsch was an early master of this, building elegantly hilarious jokes, one on top of the other, until his audience was charmed and satisfied. In *Ninotchka* (1939), a sterling example of the "Lubitsch touch," watch what comedic mileage he gets out of a hat. Greta Garbo portrays an unbending Russian envoy who has come to Paris to supervise the sale of some jewels for the benefit of the socialist republic. Upon arriving at her needlessly upscale hotel, she is already in a bad mood. She sees a window display featuring a flamboyant hat. The chapeau strikes her as a frivolous display of capitalism, and she comments darkly to her Bolshevik accomplices: "How can such a civilization survive which permits their women to put such things on their heads? *It won't be long now, comrades.*"

Passing the store again later, Ninotchka shakes her head with disdain. Even later in the film, we begin to wonder if the charms of an American suitor, Melvyn Douglas, will ever wear her down. She gives us no clue. Then one morning, Ninotchka sends away her comrades and secretly opens a drawer in her suite. Out comes the flamboyant hat. She tries it on, sternly examining her communist ideals crumbling before her in the mirror. The movie spins to giddy new heights. The idea came during a grueling writing session. Lubitsch emerged from a bathroom break and announced, "The hat is the answer."

Charles Brackett and Billy Wilder, co-writers of *Ninotchka*, looked at each other. There was no hat yet written into the script, but Lubitsch was right. The hat is the answer. The hat is everything. And it was a perfect example of the Lubitsch touch—let the audience add up two and two. Lubitsch's protégé, the treasured Billy Wilder, is among the last of the great comic writer-directors. On the wall of his small Beverly Hills office are no garish posters of his masterpieces, *Some Like It Hot, The Apartment, Sabrina* or even *Sunset Boulevard*. Just a small sign by his door, reading: HOW WOULD LUBITSCH DO IT?

Today, Lubitsch would do it not unlike modern film-comedy masters like James L. Brooks, Mike Nichols or Woody Allen. If only for the sparkling exchanges of dialogue that mark their work, each of them has long been in the big-screen comedy hall of fame. But the timeless images of their films often come not in the banter but in the devastating dialogue-free moments like Jane Craig's (Holly Hunter) daily cathartic cry in *Broadcast News*. Or in *The Graduate*, when Mrs. Robinson (Anne Bancroft) takes a puff of that cigarette, and the painfully inexperienced Benjamin (Dustin Hoffman) lunges for a kiss. He pulls away, yearning for a reaction, as Mrs. Robinson coolly exhales. It's embarrassing, it's voyeuristic, you almost shouldn't be watching . . . and it's *funny as hell*.

In the quest for fast-moving global entertainment, these days studios often trim these quiet moments. Move things along! The audience is ahead of you! The result can be catastrophic, a quicker version of less. Sometimes the audience doesn't *want* to move ahead; they'd rather luxuriate in what they *imagine* the character is thinking. Those supposedly unimportant moments often mean the world, especially in romantic comedy. In preparing to direct *Jerry Maguire,* I found a couple of movie frames that became important visual touchstones for the relationship between Jerry Maguire (Tom Cruise) and Dorothy Boyd (Renée Zellweger). The stills came from George Stevens's *Woman of the Year* (1942), freeze-frames of two simple looks between Spencer Tracy and Katharine Hepburn, sizing each other up, *regarding* each other. There was a lot of history, much of it sexual, in those looks. The stills were pasted onto the first page of my script. We often looked at them before shooting. Perhaps I overdid it. By the last few weeks of filming, when I headed over to talk to them, the actors would often see me *start* to open my script book and say: "Got it! We're gonna regard each other!" It was no empty exercise. I left most of those moments in the movie.

It's fashionable these days to say that romantic comedy is dead or dying. There are far fewer things keeping characters apart than in the days of Lubitsch, or so the theory goes. It's not true, of course. There will always be achingly funny differences between people, and *vive la différence.* Those awkward moments that we might never have expected to see on a big screen will continue to create comedy. Life is funny, it's just a matter of editing out the boring parts . . . or, hell, you can give up and go for a fart joke. That's funny, too. There will always be a glorious surprise, a happy accident that makes an audience laugh and saves a worried director's neck. It's a serious business, the honorable pursuit of those elusive moments. To quote Ernst Lubitsch himself: "A laugh is not to be sneezed at."

Cameron Crowe began his career in journalism at the age of fifteen, writing for publications including the *Los Angeles Times, Creem, Playboy,* and *Penthouse.* At sixteen, he joined the staff of *Rolling Stone* as a contributing editor, rising to associate editor as he profiled music legends like Bob Dylan, David Bowie, and Eric Clapton. At twenty-two, he returned to high school as a senior to research the best-selling book on teen life, *Fast Times at Ridgemont High.* Crowe's screenplay for *Fast Times at Ridgemont High*—his first—was nominated for a Writers Guild of America Award for Best Screen Adaptation. In 1989, he made his feature film debut as a writer/director with *Say Anything,* following it up with *Singles* in 1992. His next film, *Jerry Maguire,* released in 1996, garnered Crowe a nomination for a Directors Guild of America Award, and Academy Award® nominations for Best Screenplay Written Directly for the Screen and Best Picture. In November 1999, Knopf published Crowe's *Conversations with Wilder,* a rare series of interviews conducted with the legendary writer/director Billy Wilder. Crowe is currently in postproduction on a DreamWorks feature film due out in 2000, which was not yet titled at press time.

ROGER DIRECTOR

THE FIRST TIME my poetry received national acclaim, I was writing for a TV show in Hollywood.

The town is not known as a nursery for such laurels. What made my epic literary rise even more improbable was that I had published only two previous poems. The first was in third grade. "The night is dark, the moon is low/ The leaves wave gently to and fro" appeared in the *Tri-Town Leader* next to a discount coupon for an oil change. My budding verse ambitions played second fiddle back then to bigger dreams: convincing Brian Genson we were good enough friends for him to give me one of those eye-popping new Japanese baseball mitts his father imported. I assured Brian that I would give him one of the sofa beds my dad sold, but I couldn't fit one on my bike's handlebars to ride it over.

My second published poem was included in an anthology.

The congratulatory letter from the editor contained no pay but a priceless admonition: Keep writing! I composed the submission during my postcollege sojourn skidding a cab around ice-and-granite-bound Barre, Vermont, where my most frequent "fare" was a bottle of Wild Turkey I'd been dispatched to pick up and deliver. Housebound asthmatics, who were either too breathless or desperate for a drink to exhale a "thanks," snatched at the new arrival from behind barely opened doors. Behind my door I hunched over my desk, a wood slab balanced on cinder blocks and piles of books, looking out a farmhouse dormer window at the Green Mountains, trying to provide myself any convincing proof my future lay in writing.

My career is a quest to amass enough evidence to prove I should quit. The poetry writing may have slackened, but never the kernel urge that drew my pencil to the margin of my grade-school loose-leaf. That pure impulse, that fly-cast of words, abides within most writers, and must be protected however much circumstance or fortune assails it. Which they will, not in-frequently with your own help, oddly enough, when the quick deposit window at the ATM refuses to credit a sonnet sequence.

So, as if in some intrapersonal brawl with my soul, I tumbled over and over from one "barroom" floor to another—master's degree, newspaper, magazine, comedy revue. Until I crashed through yet another wall and glanced up to find myself in an office in California writing for TV, like so many other pursuits in a writer's life en route to penning deathless rhymes, something I'd assured myself I'd never do.

How fortunate for me, though. Building 3 on the MTM lot was television's version of the Swiss patent office. Down the hall an Einstein named Bochco had reconstituted physics with *Hill Street Blues*.

The wonderful actor Michael Conrad played the pivotal part of Sgt. Phil Esterhaus. Esterhaus was the emotional bedrock for the cops he supervised. He was also the show's structural pillar—his roll call set nearly all the stories in motion.

Tragically, Conrad fell ill. When he died, the cast and crew, and the show's fans, were at a loss. Behind closed doors at one end of the Swiss Patent Office, bulky decisions had to be made about story lines and casting. While all of that was chalked out, the immediate necessity was, as it always is, some lines. They were in a rush. There could not fail to be a church service for Sgt. Esterhaus in the next episode.

Someone had the idea that at a memorial there ought to be a poem. Maybe it was me. In any event, while others wrestled with the critical tasks of safeguarding a show—a many-headed, multi-million-dollar enterprise—a studio, a network and its ratings, stockholders and sponsors, I retreated to my office with the humblest job of all: Write the poem.

As I raced the clock and pondered in my office, I gazed past terra-cotta and palms, casting my mind toward both winter on The Hill and that winter years before by the Green Mountains, the jagged horizon I'd gazed at with such fierce speculation. I was working in the context of a life and a writing discipline that was more than a continent distant.

About a half hour after I'd finished there was a knock on my door. My boss, Steven Bochco, stuck his head in and told me he'd liked my poem very much. When the greatest writer-producer in the history of television tells you you've done okay, you can unslink a little.

Some days later, at home, in my den, I watched the TV as an actor playing a chaplain read Phil Esterhaus's poem:

I STAND AT EASE

I am at ease,
It's end of day—
My duty has been done;
The hour calls me
Far away, beyond
The setting sun.
Meet me by the ocean's rocks
In the shadows on the lane,
Find me in the snowflakes
As they crowd against the pane;
Or beckon me in silence,
Then listen to the breeze,
And you will hear me always
For at last I stand at ease.

I haven't progressed all that far since third grade. I know. Yet I've come to realize maybe that's not so bad.

Given the show's ratings, my poem was heard by 15–20 million people. This claimed for me an audience the immortal likes of Byron or Homer took centuries to reach. The numbers speak to the vast communicative power of mass media. But that, of course, is only a facetious satisfaction. The true, precious pleasure, the same as it ever was, is finding the poem inside you.

Roger Director is the author of *A Place to Fall* (Villard) and has written and produced such television series as *Moonlighting, Hill Street Blues, Mad About You,* and *Arliss.* A past recipient of the Mike Berger Award for his journalism at the New York *Daily News,* his work has appeared in a variety of publications, including *Vanity Fair,* the *New Yorker, Esquire,* and the *New York Times Magazine.* He was born in New York City and lives in Santa Monica, California, with his wife, Jan Cherubin, and daughter, Chloe.

DELIA EPHRON

THE FIRST TIME I got paid for it, I was getting paid for doing something else. In my early twenties, I had a little crochet business, making purses and belts for boutiques. Secretly, I wanted to be a writer. But since I didn't want to admit it to myself, I decided to write a crochet book about my methods and designs. Since it would be full of instructions, the only "real writing" I would have to do was the introduction, and then a few snippets here and there in the chapters. This was, I rationalized, sort of writing, but not. I sold the idea of this book at a party. I said to an editor I barely knew, "I'm sure you wouldn't want to buy this but . . ." and for some reason he agreed to buy it on the spot. I have never sold anything at a party since, and I would never ever try to pitch a movie or any other idea by saying, "I'm sure you wouldn't want to buy this but . . ." The obvious answer is, "You're right, I wouldn't." I wrote this book, and another about sewing, and by then I was admitting out loud that I wanted to be a writer.

One night, I was eating chocolate pudding my way, which involved making a little hole in the skin and scooping out the pudding underneath, and I noticed that my friend was eating it her way, which was slightly different. The next morning I wrote "How to Eat Like a Child." The article was simply a list of foods, and deadpan instructions for how children eat them: "Mashed Potatoes: Pat mashed potatoes flat on top, make several little depressions . . ." And so forth. I sold the article to the *New York Times*. It was only 500 words, so short that I forgot to retain the rights, and had to go scurrying back for them. I was offered a book contract, and the book, *How to Eat Like a Child and Other Lessons in Not Being a Grown-up,* was a best-seller, and became a TV special, as well as a children's musical theater revue. I was so naive that I thought every article I wrote would produce mountains of mail and a book contract.

It is now 20 years later. The book went out of print this year and the TV special is never repeated. The musical revue, published by Samuel French, is still put on in schools and children's theaters all over the country. Because the original article (and in fact the entire book) consisted of instructions, just like my crochet book, I believe that no writing I have ever done is a waste. And because it was funny and personal, I discovered who I was as a writer. I found my identity in 500 words about children and food.

I became a screenwriter because I married a screenwriter, and he taught me how. I had written a book called *Teenage Romance,* and CBS let me adapt it for a television movie. Every day I would come home from my office, and show my husband (whose name is Jerome Kass) what I had written and he would say, "Where's the conflict?" "Where's the drama?" And I would rewrite everything the next day. He taught me to tell a story—the reason I was then able to go on and write novels as well—and he taught me things like, if there's a problem in the third act, it probably means the problem is in the second or first act. And, to mention another favorite: Every problem is an opportunity. My television movie didn't get made, but, like many screenplays that don't get made, it was quite good. In my opinion.

Delia Ephron is a screenwriter, author, and producer. Her latest novel is *Big City Eyes*, and her latest movie is *Hanging Up*, which is based on her novel. Her other movies include *Michael* and *You've Got Mail*.

DEVERY FREEMAN

COLLABORATING WITH YOURSELF

CHARLIE LEDERER once said writing is the only job at which you can't whistle while you work. How true. In our creative incarnations, how many times have we told ourselves to shut up and write?

I envy those of you among us who write for the sheer joy of it. I fall into the Jonathan Swift mode. Every work morning he had a servant lead him to his desk and tie him into a chair.

I envy and admire those of you who write from the heart, the stomach and other bodily organs. I've never been blessed with that kind of awesome honesty. I've always had to invent myself to meet the demands of the marketplace.

As a writer of fiction in the thirties there didn't seem to have been any real me at all. I wrote with romantic passion for the women's magazines; sophisticated for the *New Yorker;* very Brit for *Punch;* macho for the pulps.

The challenge was no different for me in films. In those days when the biz was seven studios (five majors and two minors), most of us worked under the infamous seven-year contract (breakable by studio will or whim) or on week-to-week deals called assignments.

You writers who love to write and who write with uncompromising honesty will ask: "Okay, but within the strictures of an assignment was there no room for self-expression?"

Of course there was. Talent will find ways to assert itself. Honest feelings have a life of their own. But it isn't easy when the enemies are time and production demands.

A typical assignment: Paramount 1949.

Dev, we'd like you to write an original screenplay for us . . . Well, not exactly original . . . We want a sequel to Norman Krasna's *Dear Ruth* . . . You know, Bill Holden, Joan Caulfield . . . Only one thing, we can't get Bill Holden . . . Can't get Joan Caulfield either . . . Nevertheless, we'd like the feeling they're both in it . . . And, oh yes, this will be low budget. Under four hundred thousand . . . And one more thing. We've got to have it on the sound stages in six weeks . . .

I tie myself in a chair and *Dear Brat* is born to warm reviews and tidy profits. But all that becomes somebody else's business as I reincarnate myself for another week-to-week assignment, hoping to make this one last a little longer, for God's sake!

Week to week. In those days writers rarely got to the sound stages to see their scripts shot. I wrote five pictures for Red Skelton (three of them judged to be his best) and never met him. Never spoke to him. Not even on the phone.

In the fifties a television year, aside from reruns, was thirty-nine weeks. Even with six polished scripts in hand before shooting started, by midseason you were fighting to get on the boards. In those pioneer days of television, writers were being hired as producers because it was presumed we could punch up a weak script or doctor a bad one overnight and have it on the sound stages early next day.

My first assignment as a producer, *The Thin Man,* was all about time. The show was in danger of being canceled when I was asked to "save it." Only thirteen segments remaining on the schedule. How many scripts in hand? None.

Time. Precious time. Writing on the midnight shift. Daytimes rushing between office and set as shooting zoomed into golden hours. Racing to the Metro front gate to catch an actor for a wild line.

For those of you working within the strictures of today's market, new demands are being made, demands that may seriously hamper your most earnest desire to express yourself. In the quest for world markets you are being asked to write in international languages such as sex, violence, and special effects.

Nevertheless there are those among you who steadfastly keep faith with yourselves and your craft, turning out honest and artful films that charm their way into our hearts and box office success. To you dedicated writers my hat is off. Please, please don't reinvent yourselves.

In early TV days **Devery Freeman** wrote for the classic anthologies. His *Great American Hoax* won a Screen Writers Guild Award. He wrote for and produced *The Ann Sothern Show, Desilu Playhouse,* and *The Thin Man,* among others. He also wrote twenty films, some of them cult favorites. His novel *Father Sky* was adapted as the picture *Taps.*

JOHN FURIA, JR.

DON QUIXOTE DE LA NETWORK

MY FIRST SCRIPT had more lives than a cat and earned me less than a box of Kitty Litter. At CBS, in the days when the "Golden Age" of television was being replaced by the golden age of residuals, I worked as an associate producer. Don't ask me what I did. I was very young, very idealistic and reasonably ambitious. I did everything that wasn't illegal or immoral . . . to the best of my knowledge. Among the things I did was to work with agents representing the writers we hoped to employ, and then work with the writers to explain what we wanted, what our budget limitations were, and please, sir, when do you think we might have a first draft? In those hallowed times, writers were asked, not told.

I was not so dense that I failed to see the handwriting on the wall. Film made television shows repeatable, which made them more valuable, and live and taped dramas were headed for the museum. So I allowed youthful dreams to persuade me that I might be able to transmute a modest talent for short stories, polished at college, into writing for television. I presented a ninety-minute teleplay with a mountain of excuses and caveats to an agent I dealt with who had two extraordinary qualities: He was more optimistic than a guy heading into his sixth marriage, and he was utterly forthright. If he didn't think he had the right client for a job, he said so. If he didn't believe in a script, he wouldn't represent it. I thought he agreed to read mine because he respected my work. He later told me he read everything, including a script handed to him by a dental hygienist while swabbing his molars.

His name was Mel Bloom and he headed the literary department at one of the prominent agencies. Mel liked my script. He wanted to sign me. So the script went out and the following saga began. Someone liked it. I was called to a meeting, wrote a sample story. The story was turned down. The script went out again. Same chain of events. Again and again and again.

Mel never lost his jaunty confidence. My job at CBS ended and I stared in the mirror each morning trying to persuade myself that jaunty confidence would soon pay the mortgage and buy food for my wife and children. It felt as if I was caught up in a terrible dance, choreographed to test Job after the sheep were burned, the camels were stolen, the house fell in and Yahweh ran out of boils and plagues.

My job had ended around Christmas. I gave myself a year to sell something as a writer. I scrimped. I was hypnotized by the monthly reports showing my savings account flowing out like an ocean tide that only receded. My script continued to go out. Everyone liked it! I wrote countless stories and treatments. Originals. Episodes. They marched from my typewriter like the

Aussies at Gallipoli, heroic and doomed. Another Christmas approached. I was broke. Holidays, I knew, were not a fertile time for sales by unknown writers. I called everyone I knew in production and offered my services at cut rates. Not now. Maybe later. Later doesn't pay the bills. I scanned the want ads and it dawned on me that with a double major in constitutional history and philosophy, and several well-paid years in television production, I had a splendid résumé for . . . exactly nothing.

Two weeks before Christmas I applied for a job selling used cars. The hearty manager left me with the encouraging words that if I couldn't even sell myself to him, how could I sell his cars? Mel called to tell me that the producer of a new show called *The Rebel* had read my script and liked it. He wanted a story submission. The show was a Western about a young man wandering the West and encountering adventures. This was the sixties. So the hero was, by no coincidence, an outsider, a counterculture loner. I liked Westerns. But I had not the foggiest notion of what was counterculture in the Old West. Cattle were already free range. Rights for horses? Brown rice instead of beans? How the hell did I know?

Perhaps it was my desperation. Or not wanting to think of the sad faces of my children on Christmas morning. Perhaps I was beginning to hallucinate. I wrote a story about a man driven mad by the loss of his ranch and family, who slipped into the role of his favorite character from literature. He became Don Quixote, traveling the plains on his spavined horse, righting wrongs wherever his demented mind perceived them. And attracted by his nobility and his sense of justice was of course his Sancho Panza, the hero of the series, the Rebel. How's that for counterculture?

On a dreary day after New Year's, mortgage payment borrowed from a friend, I contemplated life and cursed the script I had written which had opened countless doors and encouraged me in the folly of believing I could earn a living as a writer. The phone rang. It was the ever cheerful Mel. "Happy New Year," he said, and without waiting for my tepid response: "They bought your story." I was afraid to believe him.

In the next few weeks my world turned upside down. I met with the producer who liked my Don Quixote story. He enthused about the wonders of the sample script Mel had originally shown him. He thought my story for his show was fresh and touching and had submitted it to the network. About a year later, I saw the network response. The producer had been discreet enough not to show it to me at the time. He probably didn't favor the thought of a writer committing seppuku right there in his office. "Scathing" doesn't capture the power or the nuance of the network memo. There were several comparisons with excrement. Unfavorable comparisons. There were questions as to who was more demented, the Don Quixote character or this writer. There were imputations of the fitness of this producer to find his derriere with both hands and a map. And in case the message was somehow being missed, across the bottom of the memo were two handwritten words: "No Way."

Nevertheless, something magical happened. Perhaps Satan relented and told Yahweh to leave that poor would-be writer alone. Within a few weeks I had sold another story, written the teleplay, been signed to a multiple contract. Fortune smiled. My friend got his mortgage money back. The tide came roaring in. Movies were offered. Staff positions. A year later I could pick and choose assignments.

Making that first sale changed me. At least the perception of me changed. Somewhere between enlightenment and corruption, I've never been sure. It was considerably more satisfying than trying to sell used cars.

That script? The one that opened so many doors? The one which tormented me for over a year and broke my heart so many times? It sits in my file, pristine, undaunted, defiant. But never sold. Or as Mel might say, "Not yet sold."

John Furia, Jr. is past president of both the Writers Guild of America and the Writers Guild Foundation. He has been a writer/producer of miniseries and many movies for television, a series *showrunner*, and writer of screenplays for Universal, MGM, and Columbia.

JOHN GAY

THE FIRST TIME I got paid for it was creating a series which appeared on WOR-TV's first day on the air in New York. The pay was three dollars to make the contract legal. Not three dollars for each script of the series. Or for a week or a year. Just three dollars. It also included the services of my wife and myself on the show as a struggling young married couple which we were. The scripts ran fifteen minutes five times a week prime time. When our savings disappeared and it became obvious that we couldn't go on for lack of life support, we applied to the unemployment office which notified us that we didn't qualify as we *were* employed and paid money (the three bucks) under an existing contract. It was at that dramatic moment that we informed WOR the show had a severe financial problem. Magnanimously, they came through. I can't remember the amount, but it did allow for three meals a day at Horn & Hardart plus a cold-water Village flat at twenty-five dollars a month.

Those fifteen minutes five times a week became a formidable task. After three months we mercifully mutated to a half-hour once-a-week detective format fifty-two weeks a year. A great relief. WOR brazenly called us *Mr. and Mrs. Mystery*. Unlike a *Murder She Wrote,* we could only afford four actors on each show the first few months so there wasn't much of a choice at guessing the villain. It was a daunting challenge. Later, we had not only the luxury of more actors but occasional writers. An even greater relief.

The usual live TV mishaps occurred, of course, but in our case, budget limitations made us prone to them. Dead bodies would rise with such frequency they seemed almost mandatory. What can you do with a deep cut on your hand at the very beginning of a show? It was a diamond, fake of course. The blood that flowed that night seemed equivalent to the severing of a major artery. I kept the hand in my pocket (unobtrusively?) the entire time, which brought about a crimson tide to a white summer suit. It was live TV. It was wonderful. It was . . . The Golden Age.

Even with the abysmal money, I was also required to perform commercials. The "Miller High Life" jingle will jangle in my mind forever. Not that I was forced to sing it but I did have to drink the stuff on camera. Beer brought into the studio. Warm beer. So warm. I made the discovery that a warm beer produces prolonged episodes of inescapable belching. The sponsor, naturally disturbed, decided to place the commercial at the show's conclusion.

There were three run-throughs and a dress rehearsal on the day of the broadcast. That was it. As the actors were inclined to "go up" with more frequency than they might in a well-rehearsed play, it was necessary in self-defense to learn everyone's lines. I'm prepared to say no detected pause lasted longer than five seconds on our show.

"No one knows anything." Yes, always thus. But here was a time when it was openly admitted. A medium so new that directors, writers and producers were on an almost level playing field and opportunities were abundant. When our own show's demise joined all of those dead bodies we left behind, a choice had to be made. Writing? Acting? Years of summer stock and a Broadway show pointed to the latter but I wanted to give myself an opportunity to write something other than "You'll never get away with it."

The prime-time market at the time was in dramatic anthologies of thirty minutes or one hour. I gave it a try and was surprised to be told only a week later that Lux Video Theatre was buying it. That was encouraging enough to continuing writing but the deciding factor came when I was informed Fredric March and his wife, Florence Eldridge, would star in it. With these two revered actors of the American theater and film, I was heartened to such an extent that I could almost say now THAT was the first time I got paid for it. March and Eldridge were both wonderful, of course. With one exception. At the play's conclusion, Ms. Eldridge sat at a mock dressing table and, turning directly to the TV camera, said with great feeling, "I don't know about you, but *I* always use Lux toilet soap for my skin." Yes, it was mandatory for actresses doing the show. Think, perhaps, of Glenn Close at the final moments of a Hallmark Hall of Fame declaring, "I send a Hallmark card when I want to send the very best." The Golden Age.

Half-hour dramatic shows were difficult as the given time was so limited. An editor for one of them, Charles Jackson (of *Lost Weekend* fame), told me to write the half hour as the third act of a play. Start it on a high dramatic note and never let up. Somehow it worked.

In the full-hour market, there were Philco-Goodyear, Studio One, Kraft, etc., and none of them paid enough to get you off riding subways. Kraft, I believe, came through with a magnanimous $800 a script. They ran a promotional contest one year asking their audience to vote for the best play of the year. $50,000 to the winner! I came in second. Zip.

They might have taken that $50,000 from their budget and spread it out to each of the fifty-two writers for that year. They might have? Hardly. The Golden Age did not produce much real gold. No wonder then I've been actively engaged with the Writers Guild for so many years. Forgetting the money, however (and who wants to?), live television had its upside. It was more akin to theater than to film. Not only rehearsals every day for two weeks but it wasn't unheard of for a director to actually like having the writer present. Especially *Playhouse 90,* where we had an additional thirty minutes. "90" also brought us "tape," however. Just a few minutes in each show at first to be used when a set was too elaborate for the live broadcast. Then longer tapes . . . and longer. The ultimate result was the death of live dramatic anthologies.

An agent in New York, Blanche Gaines, ran her own small agency at that time. Frank Gilroy, Rod Serling, Carey Wilbur, Arthur Hailey and others. Unfortunately, the roof caved in for her. She lost us. The work moved to the West Coast and so did we. The breakup was very traumatic for all of us. So much so in Rod's case that he wrote a *Playhouse 90* about it called *The Velvet Alley* in which Blanche was played by Jack Klugman. During the telecast, Blanche called from New York. "Not to spoil it for you, but I die at the end."

A dear lady in a remarkable time. A time of fresh openings for new writers. For me, that not only defines The Golden Age, it also designates the first time I got paid for it.

———————

John Gay has written extensively for theater, film, and television. In addition to *Diversions and Delights,* which premiered in San Francisco before a Broadway engagement at the Eugene O'Neill Theater in 1977, his theater credits include *Christophe* and *Summer Voices.* He is perhaps best known as the screenwriter of several feature films spanning the past four decades, including *Run Silent, Run Deep* (with Clark Gable and Burt Lancaster), *Separate Tables* (shared credit with Terence Rattigan), *Sometimes a Great Notion* (with Paul Newman and Henry Fonda), and *No Way to Treat a Lady* (with Rod Steiger and Lee Remick). He's also written many films for television, classics adaptations such as *Les Misérables* and *A Tale of Two Cities* and miniseries such as *Fatal Vision* and *Blind Faith.* Gay is the recipient of a Writers Guild Laurel Award, four Writers Guild Award nominations, an Academy Award® nomination, an Emmy Award nomination, a Christopher Award, a WGA Morgan Cox Award, an ACE Cable Award nomination, and an AGA Media Award.

LARRY GELBART

THE FIRST TIME?

I HAVE TO go back a couple of weeks. 1944, I think it was. That's when I got my first-ever first check as a professional writer. Forty dollars. At sixteen, it was the most money I had ever earned. I'd brought home a few bucks working weekends as a stock boy at a hardware warehouse in downtown Chicago, auditioning for a hernia, lunching among the grommets and the gadgets on mother's homemade sandwiches: chopped liver acting as mortar between brick-size slices of challah, an egg bread that is the Jews' answer to Silvercup. At 13, I had scored about three hundred in cash for my impersonation of a man at my confirmation, but that was an amateur purse. No one can make a living being a Bar Mitzvah boy. Dividing the three bills by the thousands of hours I had studied for my Super Saturday, I figure I wound up being paid about a nickel a week. Still a kid, still in Chicago, I helped turn out six-inch-high plaster figurines of General MacArthur at the Globe Auto Glass Company for ten dollars a week. You have to remember, though: In those days, ten dollars wasn't much money either.

1943. My father brought his barbering tools and family to L.A. Manifest Destiny. And who needed winters anymore? Transferring to Fairfax High School, I never dreamt that, in time, along with Mexico's Ricardo Montalban and Tijuana Brass boss Herb Alpert, I would be considered one of Fairfax's most distinguished graduates—the chief difference between us being that I could neither speak nor blow Spanish.

At 15, a completely ambition-challenged, converted Californian, I found myself reprising the role of the stock boy. Still a lowly position, but this time, I played it with a tan. My employer was the Ace Slip Cover Company at 8110 Beverly Boulevard (I was to write that on so many shipping labels it was how I would eventually sign my marriage license). My hours were: school, eight to twelve—work, one to five. For some reason, employment was treated as a school subject, although to this day I don't understand why Fairfax gave students extra credit for doing outside, nonscholastic activities. I, for one, had no intention of going on to the Ace Slip Cover College. However many useless credits I piled up, I did pocket about twenty dollars every Friday. Not a lot of swag, but I was more than compensated by the job's chief perk, which was the act of getting down on my knees several times a day to sweep under the dozen or so sewing machines, for a teen-cam view of observing the women operators pumping their legs up and down as they worked their treadles.

My father, whose barbering career was to progress from grooming the hair of Chicago neighborhood punks like Jack Ruby to doing the same for Hollywood-visiting presidents like

John F. Kennedy, took an inordinate amount of pride in the fact that I had started writing comedy material for high school productions. That is, whenever I could tear myself away from sweeping under the sewing machines over at Ace Slip Cover Prep. What made my father the proudest, I think, was that I could write anything at all. He had been trained at his craft as a twelve-year-old in Latvia, and it would be decades before he had the courage to put pencil to paper for anything other than a gin rummy score.

A combination Sweeney Todd and Mama Rose, his straight razor in hand, his chutzpah in free fall, my father zeroed in on just the right target on his celebrity client list. He arranged for me to write some sample material for comedian Danny Thomas, who was then taking his baby steps as a star, appearing weekly on a radio program starring the late Fanny Brice. (More and more, the people I write about seem to require the use of the word "late" before their name. I find the term somewhat ambiguous. After all, it's not as though these people are merely tardy and stand much of a chance of some day being referred to as punctual.) Thomas liked what I wrote, a short sketch centered around the character he played on the Brice show; liked it enough to pass me on to the show's chief writer, the late (sorry—in more ways than one) Mac Benoff. It wasn't too long before I was reporting to Mac at his house, helping to write jokes for the radio program after school every day instead of filling out mailing labels at Ace. It was a definite step up, supplying shtick instead of shipping chintz. I never questioned—I still don't—where the ability to do what I was doing came from. It seemed—it still does—to come quite naturally. Which means, of course, that it is more than possible that it will one day go just as naturally.

A couple of weeks into my apprenticeship, Mac handed me a personal check. Forty dollars. "Buy yourself a sport jacket," he said. You could get a sport jacket for forty dollars in those days. You could get a suit for a hundred. What you couldn't get, for no money, was the sort of pride I felt in the discovery that I had the ability to deliver material on demand. That, and the realization that although I was still wet with Clearasil behind the ears, I had lucked—been pushed, actually—into the kind of work that I could do happily, and perhaps even do well, for a lifetime.

Sitting at home one night, listening to a broadcast of the Fanny Brice Show, I heard a line delivered that I had written just hours earlier. A miraculous moment followed. The studio audience broke into a huge laugh. Two hundred people, not one of them a doting relative, nor an undiscriminating schoolmate, nor a co-working, treadle-pumping seamstress, were laughing. Absolutely perfect strangers were actually entertained by something that had found its way from my head into theirs.

In the third act of my life, Mac's framed check still hangs in a prominent position in my memory (right next to the cash register). But that gift from an unseen audience, the reward of their laughter way back then, in what was prologue for the next half century, will always enjoy pride of place with me.

————————

Larry Gelbart was born a writer—and has died in that capacity on more than one occasion.

GARY DAVID GOLDBERG

MY FIRST SALE

I MADE my first sale in the fall of 1975. It was of a story idea for *The Dumplings,* a short-lived TV series created by the team of Nicholl, Ross and West (who later went on to megasuccess with *Three's Company*).

I had come to Los Angeles in May of that year, tagging along semiaimlessly with my wife, who had a real reason to be here, having been accepted to the Ph.D. program in communication at USC. I thought I would kind of give writing a try between taking care of our baby (now 26!) and taking care of our dog, UBU (now our corporate logo). I dutifully watched a lot of TV, read a lot of books about writing for TV, and somehow managed to write a lot of scripts for TV, some of which people even seemed to like a little. Not enough to offer employment but enough to make me willing to go back and try again. The call from *The Dumplings* was my first actual meeting that could result in actual work with actual money changing hands and some of it actually going to me.

Bernie West, God bless him, had read and liked a spec-pilot I had written, "Free Clinic," based on my experience volunteering at the Free Clinic in Berkeley. Unbeknownst to me, Bernie's wife, Mimi, was (and is) a strong supporter and benefactor of the Free Clinic here in Los Angeles. And, the script, while not exactly "Neil Simon–Funny," cast a sympathetic and respectful eye towards everyone who worked at the clinic. So, Bernie was predisposed to look kindly on my novice effort and that's how I ended up in his office at KTTV one day in November of my thirty-first year.

What was fascinating about Nicholl, Ross and West (aside from their willingness to meet with me) was that they functioned in communication terms as a classic Three-Person Problem Solving Group. And, my wife, going for her Ph.D. in communication, as she was, was becoming something of an expert in the field of Small Group Communication in general, and Three-Person Problem Solving Groups in particular, the workings of which she understood and felt supremely confident she could predict. And she was, as she so often is, completely right.

The first thing she did was organize and position my story ideas for maximum impact. Evidently there is an ebb and flow to the dynamics of a small group meeting and there are specific "moments" in those meetings when participants are more "available" to good ideas, and what you want to do, obviously, is try to have your best ideas being pitched at those most propitious moments. In my presentation the stars aligned at story ideas number two and number seven.

As far as the dynamics of the group itself go, basically all Three-Person Problem Solving Groups operate in the same way (and NRW was no exception). In laymen's terms, as my wife explained it, they represent the "heart," the "mind" and the "blood," with each of the partners playing one of those roles.

Bernie West was the heart. That is, whatever idea I threw out, he loved it. He supported it. It was great. I was great. I bathed in his affection.

Mickey Ross was the blood. He took the idea that Bernie and I loved and pumped it up, kept it flowing, supplied "nutrients" and "oxygen," in the form of other twists and turns and characters that could perhaps be added.

Don Nicholl was the mind. He said yes or no. What else do you have? Next! He said whether they would buy it or not.

There was some overlap, of course, but mostly they stayed within those roles and it was all I could do to not jump up at one point and yell, "You guys are a sketch Three-Person Problem Solving Group and I love you for it." And, when Don bought my second idea and then my seventh, Bernie hugged me and Mickey immediately thought of thirteen different ways to do them.

As I look back on it, in point of fact, I realize all three of those men were actually the heart. They made me feel comfortable and respected from the minute I walked in the door. They were generous and helpful, clearly wanting the meeting to work out almost as much as I did. Twenty-three years later I still remember it fondly. And, I've always considered myself so lucky that my first real meeting was with people so thoughtful and considerate.

Gary David Goldberg is the creator/writer/executive producer of numerous television series including *Spin City*, *Brooklyn Bridge*, and *Family Ties*.

BO GOLDMAN

THE FIRST TIME I needed an arbitration was in the seventh grade at the Dalton School in New York City. I lost a contest to appear at the *New York Times* Youth Forum; we had been assigned an essay, "On Democracy." I had my father write mine because he knew words like "cognizant" and "sanguine." Bobby Levinson, my best friend, had procrastinated; he was in terror before class in the boys' room, he hadn't written a word, so I wrote his paper for him. When Mrs. Mukerji announced the winner, a hush, "Bobby—," I stood up. "No, no," she said, "Not Bobby Goldman, Bobby Levinson!" The latter, the real stand-up boy, announced what I had done. Sorry, too bad, and my punishment was to be sent to New York Times Hall to listen to Bobby L. participate. Excellent preparation for watching movies I would work on.

I've never been a writer, I've always thought of it as brute work: cold sweats, inexpressible tedium, relegated to outsidedness for the rest of my life. But what else can I do? How did I survive "ins" and "outs" for the Ice Capades?

"Ladies and gentlemen, Tommy Lutz doing a Triple Litz!"

"No, Goldman," says the Producer. "The stunt is a Triple Lutz. It's Litz doing a Lutz!" Arthur Godfrey, the M.C., wants me fired.

Okay, after vacating my room at the Pageant Motel, I take a walk on the boardwalk at Atlantic City. I play skee-ball, miserable and alone. But were they not golden days: Aja Zanova, the Czech champion, all six-foot-two of her in a pea green skating outfit, how does one dream up an intro? Of course . . . "The Jolly Green Giant!"

Truth is, hasn't it been toil all the way? When assigning this trivia, the Writers Guild Foundation lady said, "Have fun!" Is she crazy? One of those creatures like Pauline Kael, who confided to me, when briefly in her favor, "I love to write!" It ended before it began.

If only the first time had been the last time. Writing mash notes to Mary Jane White in the first grade, or plagiarizing a poem, "Double Play," from *Baseball Magazine* in the fifth. Miss Downes, my English teacher, told me to ascend to a seat above everybody on the wooden case of the radiator: "Bobby, this is brilliant. You are the king!" But Billy Bernhard and Larry Buttenweiser, the Lehman Brothers heirs, exposed me. Disgraced, but immediately elected, the fattest kid in the class, to play Don Quixote (not Sancho Panza as Miss Downes pleaded) because my peers were convinced I was the best actor. The Bottom to the Top.

Hasn't it always been up and down? Awards and disasters. "Don't let it bother you," Jule Styne, my producer, said of my Broadway musical as the critics damned it with faint praise. "I've had flops of every dimension." So reassuring, so prescient.

I persevered, I suppose, because every time is the first time. What's on my mind, I think, maybe I'll find out. Sometimes something, sometimes nothing. At the end of the tunnel, a mote of light: fingertips touching fingertips. Please, God, let me find a connection.

Bo Goldman won WGA and Academy Awards® for *One Flew Over the Cuckoo's Nest* and *Melvin and Howard.* He won a Golden Globe and was nominated for the WGA and Academy Awards® for *Scent of a Woman.* In 1998, he was the recipient of the WGA's Laurel (alter kocker) Award for Screenwriting Achievement.

PAMELA GRAY

THE BLOUSEMAN COMETH

THE FIRST TIME I stood outside a movie theater that was playing a movie I'd written, I felt an overwhelming urge to take a nap. Recent events were no doubt partly to blame for this—three premieres, guest appearances at film classes, a celebration party—but I suspect that the true cause of my exhaustion was the fourteen years it had taken me to arrive at that movie theater. My body seemed to be saying, "Okay, fine, we're here, you did it. *Now* can we rest?" The following "flashback sequence" is comprised of excerpts from journals I kept throughout that fourteen-year journey.

FEBRUARY 5, 1985

I've got to turn something around re: the writing. I keep saying it's time to change my life so I can make a living as a writer but I still haven't found an answer. I loved writing that play—*loved* it—but would the life of a playwright be much different than my life as a poet? I'd still be renting apartments in Oakland, I'd still be struggling every semester for part-time teaching gigs. Not to mention that you make about as much on play royalties as you do on poetry anthology royalties. *How do you make a living and get to be a writer?* Over and over the same question.

FEBRUARY 14, 1985

In Dolores Park, San Francisco. There is a woman writing at the other end of this bench; she just came over to me because she's learning English and needs help with her homework. She asked me if you *make* or *get* money and *make* or *get* progress. The sample sentence I should have given her: *I am neither making money nor making progress.*

MARCH 29, 1985

I'm obsessed with trying to find a dining room table for the Seder. I've given up on being able to afford something new; looked in the *Bay Guardian* but there were no tables in the used furniture listings. Right below "Furniture," however, under "Instruction," is an ad that says "Are you funny?" It's for a sitcom writing class in San Francisco and I'm thinking of taking it. I don't even watch sitcoms.

MAY 1, 1985

I'm obsessed and high over my script. It happened again, the same as when I wrote the play—that magical experience of suddenly being in another world and dictating, back here in *this* world, what the characters are saying. There is no other creative high that's comparable. When I really get into fantasizing about this, the excitement is overwhelming. It feels a lot like terror. I told a few people that my new goal is to try and break into television writing and they looked at me like I was crazy. I might as well have said, "I've decided to become an astronaut."

APRIL 1, 1986

I've decided to take that screenwriting class in S.F. Now I want to write everything: sitcoms, one-hour dramas, movies. I'm obsessed. It's exhilarating to know, finally, what I want to do with my life, but at the same time there's this pounding sense of urgency: I want it *now*. Turning thirty has set off alarms inside me. It's like a biological clock, but it's not about babies; it's about work.

JULY 5, 1986

I finally heard from Ruth Bennett of *Family Ties:* "This is not a script we would buy, but you have promise and talent and should send me another one." I suppose it's good news, but I was hoping for a miracle, a ticket, a gift. The messages here: (1) Trust yourself (see, you *do* have talent, you are on the right track, you're not *crazy*) and (2) It's going to be slower than you want it to be.

FEBRUARY 28, 1989

The Scarcity Mentality Domino Game: If I don't sell a script and if I don't break in I'll never have enough money and I'll never have a stable income and I'll never get my house in the country and I'll never be a full-time writer and I'll never be happy and I'll never be where I want to be.

MARCH 16, 1990

YES. That's the answer—YES. Arms full of groceries, my hands shaking as I opened the letter: I got into the MFA Screenwriting Program at UCLA. I'm moving to Los Angeles.

DECEMBER 5, 1991

I had my notes meeting with Prof. Hal Ackerman on my first draft of *The Blouse Man*. He said, "I think you can go all the way with this one." I don't even know exactly what he meant by that (and was afraid to ask), but I loved hearing him say it. He then proceeded to tell me the million things I have to do for the rewrite.

NOVEMBER 3, 1992

My first day as a Goldwyn winner. I am so overwhelmed by everything. At moments today, I just wanted to burst into tears. Gorgeous flowers all over the house. Went to the gym and came back to eleven more phone calls. I nearly fainted when I saw the *Reporter* headline on page 6: GOLDWYN GOES TO BLOUSE MAN. And *Variety:* GRAY TOPS GOLDWYNS, with my name also on the back page under FIRST PRIZE. I bought seventeen copies!

DECEMBER 15, 1992

Another meeting telling me how talented I am "but this isn't the kind of movie our studio makes." I have to trust that this is all leading where it's supposed to. Sam Goldwyn doesn't want me to get my hopes up—the only Goldwyn-winning script that ever got produced was *Harold and Maude*. When I heard this, my heart sank, but at the same time, it makes me even more determined. In 1993 I want: to sell *The Blouse Man*, to see it green-lighted, to be working as a screenwriter. I want assignments. I want my house in the country. I want to feel like I'm just where I should be in my life, not on my way to being somewhere. The problem with L.A. is that my whole existence here is future-oriented.

NOVEMBER 15, 1993

Too soft, too small, not enough edge. They should put that on my tombstone. Everyone loves the script; no one will buy it. Everyone tells me I'm talented; no one will hire me. Here are my other favorites: *It's not universal enough; we already have our woman's movie; can you make the husband the main character?; too ethnic; Jewish movies don't make money; women's movies don't make money;* and the best one of all: *Does it have to be about Jews in the Catskills in the sixties?*

JANUARY 9, 1994

This is what I feel like:

1. I'll never clean my house
2. I'll never lose weight

3.   I'll never get a job
4.   I'll never buy a house in the country
5.   I'll never sell *The Blouse Man*

MARCH 2, 1994

My meeting with Tony Goldwyn was wonderful; he's very smart, very down to earth, and has such passion for the project. He's interested in producing the movie and possibly playing Walker. I assumed he called me because his father gave him the script, but, in fact, he knew nothing about my winning the Goldwyn Award. Coincidence.

MAY 19, 1995

Back from Kinko's, copying yet another treatment for yet another producer who's going to keep having me work on it for free and in the end not buy it. How long can I keep this up? My acupuncturist pitched to a one-hour drama and was hired on staff the next day. Where is my break? Why can't I get one? I feel doomed.

APRIL 10, 1996

How low can you go? There I was at dinner, asking my brother to find some way to create a job for me in his casket business. As I went on and on about how miserable this career [*sic*] is making me, and about all the "leads" that have led to dead ends (no pun intended), the guy at the next table said to me, "Sorry for eavesdropping, but I just want to say that I have a feeling I'm gonna be seeing your name someday." Where? In an article about wanna-be screenwriters who wind up selling caskets?

SEPTEMBER 9, 1996

I came home to a message from Tony: "I have some good news for you—I think. Dustin Hoffman's company wants to make a deal on *The Blouse Man*." Cautiously optimistic. Is this it? I'm afraid to believe anything.

MARCH 5, 1997

Cocktail party last night—I met Dustin Hoffman. When I walked in (late, by the way—so nervous I couldn't find my car keys) and saw that they'd made a mock poster for the movie (*The Blouse Man* was written around a guitar and dove, as in the old Woodstock logo), it started to hit me that this may, in fact, really be happening.

APRIL 22, 1997

> *Red light green light one-two-three*
> *Red light green light one-two-three*
>
> —BROOKLYN STREET GAME, circa 1963

It's like everyday is my birthday, or like I'm pregnant. *Blouse Man* got a green light.

July 5, 1997

I am en route to Montreal for THE PRODUCTION OF *THE BLOUSE MAN*. Village Road Show says we have to change the title. Somebody thought *The Blouse Man* was a superhero, in Asia, men who sell blouses are gay, etc., etc. They want me to use a song title. I found out that someone there has been sending the script out with the title *Light My Fire*. Ugh.

July 7, 1997

I met Jess Platt today—the dialect coach—and we became fast friends. When I told him it was my first time on a movie set and I didn't know what to expect, he pointed outside and said, "See that grass? Watch it grow." I argued that since it was my first movie—my baby—I probably wouldn't be bored. His look said, *you'll see.*

July 13, 1997

Tomorrow is the first shoot date, aka the First Day of Principal Photography! I created it, imagined it, wrote it—and it begins to be a movie tomorrow. A movie that will be in the movie theaters! Unreal. I find myself focusing on minutiae, e.g., the mah-jongg tiles aren't yellow enough. (The costume designer's mother is shipping us her set from Florida.) I love the bungalow colony Dan Leigh created; it's so strange and wonderful to see both my movie and my childhood materialized. I love seeing the sign for "Casting for Woodstock"; the yellow *Blouse Man* road signs on the highway; the pictures up of all the actors with the character names beneath them. Selma Levitsky exists!

July 23, 1997

Okay so maybe Jess is right. I am EXT. BUNGALOW COLONY—DAY, and the periods of waiting are deadly. The intermittent reinforcement, however, is all-powerful—those precious moments of watching them shoot a scene. The word made flesh. Fifteen, twenty incredible minutes, then ninety minutes of setting up for the next shot. And the ultimate reinforcement—dailies. The luminous faces of the actors, scenes beautifully shot and lit, the amazing sets and scenery—I feel that rush all over again.

July 25, 1997

Didn't like dailies tonight and the topper was seeing the hideous title list that the title company submitted. How about *The Ballad of Marty and Pearl*? Or *Lay Lady Lay*? Someone got paid to think of those. Anna Paquin's mom came up with a title: *She Schtups to Conquer*.

October 4, 1997

The Blouse Man—which will be announced in the international edition of *Variety* on Monday as *Over the Moon* (ugh)—is being edited at this very moment.

March 4, 1998

I'm sitting at the Urth Cafe with copies of the trades and the headlines: MIRAMAX BUTTONS UP RIGHTS TO 'BLOUSE' PIC and MIRAMAX FINDS 'BLOUSE MAN' TAILORED TO

FIT. I'm very excited. Scared too—each victory is another level of losing control of my baby—but it's still my baby.

APRIL 29, 1998

Went to N.Y. for the test screening. I loved hearing the women talking about it in the bathroom. One said to me, "I thought the movie was great, didn't you?" And actually, I did. There are still things I'm not happy with, but I'm starting to love the film. Now they want to change the title to *Summertime*. Ugh.

AUGUST 17, 1998

They changed the title to *Kiss the Sky* which has nothing to do with the film. I hate the trailer too. It's the same thing all over again: I have no control and I can't stand it.

SEPTEMBER 2, 1998

Giddily brainstorming titles with Tony, Dustin, et al., at a pizzeria before the Westchester screening: *Screwing, Pearl's Jam, Titanic Pearl, Oral Sex for the First Time, Pearl Diving*—and my contributions: *The Blouse Whisperer* and *Good Will Schtupping*. Then suddenly, after the screening, Harvey said yes to *A Walk on the Moon*. I did a double take; Tony and I have both been suggesting that title since last summer, and everyone has said no every time. I still want it to be *The Blouse Man*, but I can live with this second choice. At least it's poetic, at least it has layers, and at least it has something to do with the movie!

October 21, 1998

Goldwyn Awards ceremony on Monday—a strange and wonderful experience to be back there as one of the judges—and as a "success." I was reliving the way my heart was pounding six years ago in that room.

January 27, 1999

I am on my way to Sundance for the World Premiere of *A Walk on the Moon*. An internal voice keeps saying *this is it*—which unfortunately is what DiCaprio says in *Titanic* just before the ship is about to stand straight up and go under. Sink or swim.

January 31, 1999

Standing ovation on Friday night in the 1,300-seat (sold out!) theater. I started to cry when I saw the audience stand up and was still crying when I headed onto the stage for Q&A. I was terrified before the screening—could hardly bear it. But once in the world of the movie, the 1,300 anonymous judges receded and I was home again.

March 26, 1999

There it was, on the marquee of the Mann Theater on the 3rd Street Promenade: A WALK ON THE MOON. I stood to the side of the box office and watched to see if anyone was buying tickets for it. Let's put it this way—crowds aren't exactly flocking to it. But there *were* some people buying tickets, and I got to hear the words "Two for *A Walk on the Moon.*" I always thought this would be one of the most exciting moments of my life, but I am *so* tired and just want to sleep. I feel like I've sent the characters off to college—they're on their own now, out there in movie theaters without me.

Pamela Gray is the writer of *A Walk on the Moon* and *Music of the Heart.* She is currently writing *Sara,* a woman's Holocaust story, for Universal, with Agnieszka Holland attached to direct. Pamela lives in Sonoma County in a house in the country.

DEAN HARGROVE

THE FIRST TIME I actually worked at a major studio was at MGM in the early 1960s. A writer just turned producer, William Roberts, had been given the assignment to develop a few screenplays and then hopefully produce them. William Roberts was a very successful screenwriter with some very important screen credits and also very much a gentleman. After an anxious interview, I was given a writing assignment on one of these nascent feature projects. I was only twenty-two and hadn't written much, but then they weren't paying much, either. It seemed like a reasonable arrangement.

He screened a picture for me called *I Married a Witch* starring Fredric March and Veronica Lake, with a screenplay by Robert Pirosh, Marc Connelly and Dalton Trumbo. The creative strategy was to do a more contemporary version of this sort of story. Not exactly this story, since United Artists owned *I Married a Witch* and MGM didn't, but a screenplay with most of the same elements, only better, if possible.

I was assigned a small office in the middle of a long hallway in the Thalberg Building. The other offices were unoccupied as MGM was being administered by interregnum management, later to become its permanent corporate style.

The office had a desk, a chair, a lamp and a typewriter. Mr. Roberts's secretary (as assistants were known in these more primitive days) managed to find me typing paper, several lined yellow tablets and a few unsharpened pencils. Using my own native resourcefulness, I managed to sharpen the pencils and was then ready for my career as a studio writer for hire.

Unfortunately, work progressed slowly on this project. I didn't know how to structure a story and Mr. Roberts, by necessity, had to do most of the heavy thinking, for which I was very grateful. After each story session, I was sent away to my cubicle to make progress. Some days I actually did. Mostly I didn't, and since there were other demands on Mr. Roberts's time, things moved at a glacial pace.

After a few weeks of this, the studio informed my agent that I would have to finish the story treatment by the following Friday. Since I was on a flat deal, if I went another week, I would be working for less than WGA scale. The studio wasn't prepared to raise my salary to cover this contingency, so I feverishly completed the treatment.

It was dutifully delivered on a Friday and I spent the weekend in anticipation of the studio's reaction, running various congratulatory scenarios through my mind.

On Monday, when I arrived at my office, I discovered that my few personal belongings had seemingly vanished, the office having been returned to its original monastic state. I went to Mr. Roberts's office where he diplomatically told me the studio had elected not to go forward, for various reasons. I didn't ask for the reasons, as I suspected they had something to do with the quality of the material, and I thanked him for his patience and slunk off.

A disinterested studio guard led me to the basement of the Thalberg Building, where behind a chain-link screen, we discovered, among other artifacts, my personal items in a cardboard box.

With the box under my arm I crossed the parking lot to my car, realizing even then that I had been taught a valuable lesson. You'd better learn how to write a story, or your things wind up in a cardboard box.

Writer/producer **Dean Hargrove** includes *It Takes a Thief, Columbo, McCloud, The Man from Uncle,* and *The Bob Newhart Show* on the early half of his résumé. During the last several television seasons he served as writer and/or executive producer of over twenty television movies and the series *Diagnosis Murder, Matlock, Jake & The Fatman,* and *The Father Dowling Mysteries.*

JAMES V. HART

THE FIRST TIME I MET FRANCIS FORD COPPOLA

I WAS LATE and I had the runs. And, I was lost. Literally. Somewhere on a winding road along the Russian River from Santa Rosa to the Napa Valley I would meet my fate. I would never reach the Coppola estate. I would never be received in the Hall of the Godfather King and learn at the feet of the Man and force who had made it possible for Outsiders like myself to enter the realm of the celluloid guillotine. My gastrointestinal turmoil would force me off the road in search of a tree to hide behind. I would be devoured by ravenous Wolves, thus ending my fifteen-year journey to bring *Dracula* to the screen inches from the finish line. Unless of course the Wolves smelled "Screenwriter" and therefore deemed I was too low on the food chain to waste the effort.

Courage. Work on self-esteem.

My wife, son, and daughter had traveled from New York for

winter break and were anxiously waiting with the in-laws in Santa Rosa hoping for good news. Fourteen months earlier, my agency of ten years had politely informed me that "no one wants to be in the Jim Hart business." No other talent agency in or trying to be in the business would sign me: "over forty," "unproduced," "difficult," and oh, yes, "difficult."

I received this bit of news while writing *Hook,* based on my son's idea when he was six years old, and *Dracula* based on Bram Stoker's luscious gothic novel and over a hundred other movies. The Count and Peter Pan had caused many doors to be slammed in my face. "Grownups can't fly," and "Dracula sucks" is the *TV Guide* version of all related pitch meetings I had suffered in two decades.

The answer to my son's question, "What if Peter Pan grew up?" was being answered even as I tried to maintain maximum pucker factor turning up the drive to the Coppola spread. Steven Spielberg had commenced principal photography in L.A. on *Hook* with lots of pirates, a reluctant faerie/pixie, a grown-up Peter Pan, and a very large budget.

A few weeks after this announcement, Zoetrope announced *Bram Stoker's Dracula* as their first production for Francis Ford Coppola, with a writer's nod to Winona Ryder for getting the legend to read my script. Two cinema giants in the same year directing screenplays nobody wanted by an over-forty unproduced writer and both cover pages had my name on them! It was not what I ate for breakfast that was erupting in my tumload. I was about to have my question answered, a question that strikes fear into me even to this day—everyday:

"Will this be another short meeting?"

Courage. Work on forming complete sentences.

Coppola's captain's house built in the 1880s on the original Inglenook estate loomed ahead. I suddenly had a sense of how Martin Sheen felt as he sailed up the river through the smoke to Marlon Brando's heavily guarded world in *Apocalypse Now*. My adrenaline surge was no doubt identical to Al Pacino's as he approached the hospital where Brando lay unguarded in *The Godfather*.

If life is a movie, I was in a really cool one. Scared. Excited. And, in desperate need of a relief facility.

The library, my destination, is a barn with three levels. Video and reference on the first level. Upstairs a state-of-the art mixing/dubbing room which sits directly above the wine-aging room. The aromas and bouquets permeating the facility create a most civilized work space but also defines Francis's description of Zoetrope as the "bohemian Amblin."

Anahid, a formidable woman with a Ph.D. in library science, who has "typed" every script Francis had been involved in for the past ten years, greets me with her piercing eyes.

My heart rate crashes when she tells me that Francis is not there. This sensation is followed by an army of butterflies invading my pillaged gut as she continues saying Francis is waiting in the bungalow.

She calls on the intercom to him. The Man. The Renaissance Artist who pioneered the careers of George Lucas, Carrol Ballard, Al Pacino, resurrected Brando, spawned brilliant family talent like his own nephews, Nicolas Cage, now Jason Schwartzman, sister Talia Shire, daughter Sofia, and son Roman; the inventor of modern independent cinema with his hit-and-run mobile studio on wheels, developed electronic video systems in editing and production now taken for granted by every film school grad student. And who had won Academy Awards® both as director and screenwriter. This same Man was waiting to see me??!!

Courage. Use the force. Think happy thoughts. Do not break wind—

Anahid does her best to calm me down, asking about my family, about how *Hook* is going—every muscle and nerve ending in my body wants to bolt for the trees as we approach the bungalow.

"Will he remember me?" I ask myself as we enter the back door. "Do I dare mention it?" Suddenly I flash to summer, 1970. A Ford Econoline van in the middle of Utah heading for California. My filmmaker colleague from college and I were going to meet Francis Ford Coppola. Hey, we had made a film. He would want to see us and embrace us. We sat in the American Zoetrope lobby for two days staring at the octopus espresso machine. Yes, he had seen our film and yes he knows you are waiting. He is very busy. Finally, it happens. We stand as he exits his office on a Friday afternoon, takes one look at us and turns the other way. We follow.

"Mr. Coppola? We're the guys from Texas?"

"Oh? Good—"

"Did you see our film?"

"Yes."

"Well, what do you think? Can you give us some advice?"

"Keep making movies."

And, he was gone—

Gobsmacked. I dined on that moment for the next twenty years. Francis Coppola told me to "keep making movies."

So, I lied. This was not the first time I met Francis Ford Coppola. Now I was sitting across from him twenty years later watching his thick stubby fingers dance across an early notebook computer as if each digit had a ballet slipper on the tip. A statue of Goethe behind me, his muse, and deity, I suspect.

"I really said that?"

He glanced at me, opening my screenplay, a conductor about to commence a symphony. For the next two and a half hours I sat at the Master's feet as he went through my screenplay page by page telling me, painting me, mesmerizing me with the images, "the erotic fever dream of a movie" he would turn those words into.

With each passing scene and sequence, I was overwhelmed with how many of the storytelling techniques I had stolen from Coppola's greatest cinematic hits. I started laughing, embarrassed at the irony of the situation. I explained that this scene came from *Godfather*, this one from *Apocalypse Now,* that moment is from *GFII*, oh, there's a bit of *The Conversation*—

Francis smiled at me over his glasses—a mischievous professor—

"My father, Carmine, taught me a very valuable lesson. He said—steal from the best."

Courage. Steal from the best.

I did.

And, I am proud of it.

Thank you, Francis, for being the best.

James V. Hart grew up in Texas on drive-in movies and Saturday matinees. His writing credits include *Bram Stoker's Dracula,* which he also co-produced with director Francis Ford Coppola; *Hook,* screenplay and screen story with Malia Scotch Marmo and Nick Castel, directed by Steven

Spielberg; *Muppet Treasure Island,* directed by Brian Henson, screenplay with Jerry Juhl and Kirk Thatcher; and *Contact,* directed by Robert Zemeckis, screenplay with Michael Goldenberg. He produced *Mary Shelley's Frankenstein* with Francis Ford Coppola and John Veitch, directed by Kenneth Branagh. Hart's projects in development include *Jack and the Beanstalk* with CBS and Paramount for the Henson Company; *Ohio: Thirteen Seconds at Kent State* with Lovespell and Jennifer Love Hewitt for John Davis and Common Grounds Entertainment; and *The Snow Goose* with Jude Law for Daybreak Productions.

CHARLIE HAUCK

BREAKING IN BY BREAKING OUT

I ALWAYS WANTED to write, and I always had a bent for comedy, but it took me a while to bring the two inclinations together. I spent the years immediately after college in my native Cleveland taking any writing-related job that was offered to me. As a result, over a period of a few years, I was a proofreader for the *Wall Street Journal,* an editor on a welding magazine, a publicist for a cultural foundation, and an escort for General Electric's Lady of Light, whom I took around the country and booked on women's television shows, where she spoke on the benefits of electric light. I generally tried to instill a little humor into whatever I wrote, though the welding magazine was a particular challenge.

By the early 1970s, I was the bureau chief for *Business Week* magazine in Pittsburgh, where I was widely acknowledged to be one of the funniest people covering the coal, steel, and aluminum industries. Getting laughs from the *Metals Week* guy while we toured a new Jones and Laughlin pickling tank had its satisfactions, but I longed for more. And there was the matter of money. I was the father of four young children. When my youngest were born, twin sons, a colleague said to me, "Hauck, do you realize you're breeding yourself out of a decent standard of living?" College tuitions loomed like long-winged raptors flapping in the distance. I thought I might capitalize on my *Business Week* savvy to make money in investments. I gave a respectable sum to a professor of economics at Carnegie-Mellon University who had devised a way to speculate sensibly in the commodities market. He had written a book on the subject that was very favorably received. Within a year and a half, he had pyramided my $5,000 investment into $320. As I recall, it was plywood futures that did me in.

To supplement my income, I began appearing occasionally on a local public television news show doing business reports. The reports tended to be funny. Eventually the station offered me a full-time job. I was to appear on the show nightly, reporting on events of the day from a skewed angle. In effect, I was being paid to be funny. Public television is generally not the answer to the question, "How do I make a lot of money?" But for the first time I was doing something aligned with my enthusiasms. None of the business and technical jobs I'd taken up until then had been a comfortable fit.

I developed a slight reputation in public television circles. The PBS station in San Francisco offered me an on-the-air job. If I'd continued on that path, perhaps today you would occasionally hear Jim Lehrer say, "And also tonight, Charlie Hauck offers a wry look at the famine in Chad." But I had another set of duties at the Pittsburgh station—writing and producing documentaries and specials. The job offer from San Francisco came shortly after I'd won a grant from the 3M Company to produce a national PBS special aimed at the relatives of alcoholics. It was a somber topic, but the show would use humor, music and dramatic sketches to get its points across. Celebrities were eager to participate. I'd just secured Carol Burnett as the host. I realized that my true enthusiasm was for behind-the-scenes work, writing and producing. And I liked the show business aspects of the special. I'd always felt like a bit of a fake doing the news; whenever I was on the air, the voices of Bob and Ray reverberated in the back of my head. I elected to stay in Pittsburgh.

While I worked on the alcoholism special, two separate experiences coincided to send me off in a new and original direction. Perhaps, because it happened in Pittsburgh, an appropriate analogy would be how the Monongahela and the Allegheny join together to form the mighty Ohio. The first was a meeting with Phyllis Diller. For a health care project I was producing, I tried to lure every prominent comedian who passed through Pittsburgh into performing health-related comedy spots I wrote. Phyllis Diller was one of those who agreed. She was very complimentary about my material. "Do you know what you would have if you went out to Hollywood?" she said. "A swimming pool." A few days later, as I was painting my daughter's bedroom, I heard Pat McCormick, a writer for the *Tonight Show,* being interviewed on the radio. I knew about McCormick, we were fellow Clevelanders. As he talked about the mechanics of putting together a Johnny Carson monologue, and with Phyllis Diller's encouragement fresh in my ears, a daring thought struck me. I could do that. I could go out to Hollywood and write comedy. Not particularly profound, as lightning bolts go. But it did the job for me. It gave me the courage to break out of the safe life I was leading and go after something I really wanted.

When you make an authentic, heartfelt decision the whole world suddenly seems to take you seriously. A series of coincidences came to the support of my new goal. One of the writers of *Blazing Saddles,* who was in Pittsburgh to promote the movie, put me in touch with his New York agent. I wrote a *Bob Newhart* script for the agent, and he liked it. He sent it to people in Los Angeles; some of them liked it. I was about to leave for Los Angeles to tape Carol Burnett's segments for the alcoholism special at CBS Television City, but I was only going to be there for two days. But as my plane's wheels touched down at LAX, some CBS technicians went on strike; I was in L.A. for two weeks, waiting to do my taping. This gave me an opportunity to meet people who liked my *Newhart* script (none of those people, by the way, included the producers of *The Bob Newhart Show;* their reaction to my effort was on the hostile side). A script editor on *Maude* passed my script along to the producers. They liked it, but didn't know how I would do with a *Maude* script. They suggested I write a single *Maude* scene, a novel idea. When I got back to Pittsburgh, I sent them an eight-page scene. While I was in New York doing a mix on the alcoholism special, my agent called to say the *Maude* people liked the scene. If I went out to Los Angeles, they would give me a script to write.

On October 26, 1974, as the alcoholism special was airing on PBS, my plane left Pittsburgh for Los Angeles. When I arrived, the people at *Maude* were too busy to see me. Someone wrangled me an appointment with the executive producer of a Flip Wilson special that was about to begin production. Incredibly, he put me on his writing staff. He told me later that he had hired me because he was in Alcoholics Anonymous, and he had liked the show I did with Carol Burnett. While I worked on the Flip Wilson staff, I got the assignment for a *Maude* script. I worked on it at night, pounding it out on an Olivetti portable in my efficiency apartment on Larrabee Street in West Hollywood. I finished it and sent it in. A week later, while I was on an NBC stage watching Diahann Carroll rehearse "You Make Me Feel Like a Natural Woman," a page called me to the phone. It was Bob Schiller, a producer of *Maude.* He said, "I have some good news and some bad news. The good news is, Norman Lear read your script and he liked it. The bad news is, he wants to hire you." (Bad news because of the long hours his writers worked.)

I received the going rate for that first script, I think it was $6,500 in those days. More importantly, I was on the writing staff of a top television show. My career was launched. I could bring my family out

I'm happy to report, all my children have gone to college. And I do, in fact, have a swimming pool.

Charlie Hauck has created and produced seven half-hour comedy series for network television. He is currently a consulting producer on *Frasier.* His novel on the world of television comedy, *Artistic Differences,* is being made into a movie for Showtime.

GEORGIA JEFFRIES

FUNNY, YOU DON'T LOOK LIKE A . . .

THE FIRST TIME they told me I write like a man I accepted it as the tribute I knew it to be. Which—in retrospect—was my first lesson in gender perspective within The Industry. Because, if I *were* a man, such a comment would not have made sense at all. "Of course, I write like a man. I *am* a man. How else would I write?"

But I am a woman. So, to be told I write like one of God's other creatures implied a special power . . . a passport to travel to a distant realm where the border guards only admitted those native born. Still, I was curious. How exactly did a man write? I gathered clues in meetings with the executives who had voiced respect for my work. They applauded the "edge," the "passion," the "sharp" dialogue, and the occasional (but never gratuitous) uninhibited exchange of four-letter obscenities. I see. To write like a man means articulating righteous rage and other kick-ass emotions. (One might even say, expressing one's feelings.)

The executives would study me with curiosity and remark, with a touch of uneasiness, you don't *look* like what you write. Meaning, I thought, you don't look like a Marine (or Brooklyn cop or black sharecropper or child molester or drug-crazed killer or any of the other assorted dramatic protagonists I created in my screenplays). So I hastened to dispel their confusion with colorful stories of my in-field research. The days spent chasing the dust of exhausted Army recruits at Fort McClellan, the all-night patrol riding shotgun in Inglewood with a very wired police sergeant, the back-roads adventures from Mobile to Memphis, the smoke-choked Vegas bounty hunters' convention at (where else?) the Mirage, the L.A. County Jail's decided lack of amenities for alleged murderers and their note-taking guests . . .

Without exception the executives would then smile, ask a seemingly sincere question or two and move on to their own agenda. Relaxed. Reassured. Relieved that indeed I was not some suspicious anomaly of my gender. I had simply visited male worlds and returned with tales to tell. How clever of me to venture forth then share what I had seen and heard and had confided to my tender bosom. Plus a timely marketing ploy to boot.

Or, as a female colleague remarked in 1985 as we were both breaking and entering the rarefied echelons of hit television drama, "It's hip to hire women writers now." Notice the verb "hire" as opposed to "work with" or—dare I go there?—"work for." Did I mention my former colleague quit the business to become an acupuncturist? I leave it to you to draw the metaphorical analogy. Blocked energy meridians are, after all, a much healthier target to stab than voodoo dolls attired in Armanis.

It took several years of sitting on plush chairs in those well-appointed executives' offices before I truly understood what both intrigued and unnerved their sensibilities. All my characters—both the male heroes with feet of clay and the strong but ("Can't you make her more sympathetic?") flawed heroines—spilled their angry guts across the page when injustice demanded it. Those acts of courage took time to build, of course. That is the journey of any story. The price of admission for the thrills and chills of the ride does not come cheap. The insults, the injuries, the first-act struggles, the second-act defeats, the tensions that simmer to the boiling point. And finally, the confrontation, the climax, the release. Each of my protagonists ultimately was a fighter who refused to look the other way and be silenced. And how could a woman write a tough-minded warrior who slew dragons in the primeval jungle instead of cockroaches under the kitchen sink?

Indeed. In a male-owned-and-operated entertainment universe it does require imagination to step beyond conventional boundaries. A writer's imagination. With that you can actually create—voilà!—a TDC (Three-Dimensional Character), aka an intrepid Somebody not solely defined by cultural expectations. This Somebody has the capability to command respect and compassion and might even inspire the perceptive ones in the audience to look, not just at the screen, but at their own troubled, tragic, funny, and wondrous lives. Words are these characters' weapons, finely sharpened scalpels designed to sever the illusions and polite lies that society requires of those who play politics.

TDCs are dangerous folk precisely because, when they do wake from their sleepwalk, they are mad as hell. (God bless Paddy Chayefsky.) Not only do they refuse to take it—whatever "it" was—now they are frothing at the bit in their eagerness to tell the truth and undo the abusive powers that be. Pow! Slam! Bam!

Boxing for Buddha. Jousting for Jesus. Garrotting for the Goddess . . . (Before I sink in a sea of alliteration, a word from our sponsor on the issue of artists' responsibility in the prevention of violence: Writers everywhere, plug in your laptop and vent your heart out.)

In these politically correct times I find the executives no longer tell me I write like a man. Maybe they've learned that power and passion and active verbs have no gender (or class or race or national origin for that matter). Maybe not. I suspect that is a daily battle still being fought by every writer who refuses to be limited or pigeonholed. It does not really matter what "they" think after all.

What I know now is that I write exactly like a woman.*

———————

Georgia Jeffries is a WGA Award—winning writer-producer of such successful dramas as *China Beach, Cagney & Lacey,* and *Sisters*. She has also created a score of brilliant, well-paid, but as yet unproduced pilots, features, and movies-for-cable. She is currently plotting her second novel and next career move.

*And a black attorney . . . and a Jewish teamster . . . and a Latino lobbyist . . . and a British journalist and . . . any other character I put on the page. Even a man.

AMY HOLDEN JONES

THE FIRST TIME I had to write a script was also the first time I got drunk. I was twenty-seven years old. I know what you're thinking. Why, in the world, did she wait so long to get drunk? That's another, much sadder, story. Let's take them one at a time. I was about to direct my first feature for Roger Corman's New World Pictures, *Slumber Party Massacre*. The plot was straightforward, the genre familiar. Buxom girls and their callow boyfriends are menaced and then dispatched by a nut with a great big drill.

Believe it or not, I'd gotten myself into this situation without ever reading the script. Hey, it was a feature. I was going to be a director! Wasn't that the idea? I was young and apparently dim-witted. I got drunk when I read the script. I ended up flat on the floor, clutching my first bottle of gin. Disaster and public humiliation loomed. Someone had to restructure, add characters, inject humor, jump scares, more bodies and, of course, a few brilliant directorial flourishes. But who? The original writer was out of the question since, in my raw hubris, I'd promised to make *Slumber Party Massacre* for less than Roger had spent on a picture in years. Nothing was left in our pathetic budget to pay a real writer to write. I'd gone to film school and made documentaries. I was a union editor. I had never, in my entire life, pretended I could write. As I lay on the floor with the ceiling rolling and turning above me, my first thought was "I hope I don't throw up." My second was, "I can't do this." But I had no choice.

I had several things going for me in my maiden attempt at screenwriting. The bar in this particular genre was not high. *Slumber Party Massacre* did not require Harold Pinter. There are no opportunities for deep thoughts, symbolism, heartfelt soliloquies, or arch dialogue when you have to deliver a body a reel. The hard work had already been done by the original writer. I had the rudiments of a three-act structure and a theme. "What is that nasty man with the great big drill going to do to me" = fear of getting laid for the first time. Finally, the material turned out to be right up my alley. *Slumber Party Massacre* was a chick flick in disguise.

All these things combined to keep my worst instincts in check, and in four weeks I had a script. Roger read it and summoned me to his office. I was prepared for the worst. To my utter surprise he told me, "Amy, you can do this, you can write." I took it with a grain of salt. This was the producer of *The Brain Eaters* talking. Nonetheless, it felt great. In retrospect, I don't believe I've ever gotten such a clean, positive response again. The icing on the cake, or perhaps in this case, the cherry in the Shirley Temple, was Roger gave me no notes. Let's repeat that, no notes.

Slumber Party Massacre was shot exactly as it came out of the typewriter, in twenty fun-packed days. The crew was young and incredibly hardworking. The cast was cheap and willing to take their clothes off. What more could a young writer-director ask?

Several months later we previewed in the tackiest theater on Hollywood Boulevard. The place was packed with half-drunk teenagers and homeless people who walked in off the street—our target audience. The picture started and I probably would have bolted in sheer terror, but my feet were stuck to the soda and ancient dried candy on the floor. A few minutes into the film, the audience had a dead body and a nice, prolonged scare. That reassured them quite a bit. Before long, people all around me were getting into the picture, hooting and hollering and talking back at the screen. We got our biggest laugh from the dialogue of the slumber party attendees in diaphanous teddies as they checked out the body of the dead pizza delivery boy. The first girl touched him sadly. "He's so cold!" she wisely observed. Her buddy was more pragmatic. "Is the pizza?" she replied. Every burst of violence brought waves of raucous cheers and laughter. The guy behind me kept making noises like a drill. At the end of this near-death experience, I staggered out to the lobby thinking, "What have I done?" There stood Roger Corman, beaming. "Congratulations, Amy," he said. "This is our best preview in years!"

Roger made a fortune with *Slumber Party Massacre*. I hauled down less than minimum wage. The reviews were cruel. Feminists took particular offense that a WOMAN would direct this kind of exploitation movie, ignoring the fact that most men, including the likes of Jonathan Demme and Martin Scorsese, started in the business with Roger Corman, too. I spent the next six months unemployed. Finally, out of sheer boredom and desperation, I sat down and did that wonderful thing only writers can do. I wrote my first original script. It was called *Love Letters,* and it was a shade pretentious, heartfelt, full of speeches, and inspired by the screenplays of Harold Pinter. Perhaps it isn't up to the high standard of *Slumber Party Massacre,* but I'm still proud of it, and to this day it remains the only art film Roger Corman ever produced.

———

Amy Holden Jones has written and directed four features. Among her screenwriting credits are *Mystic Pizza, Maid to Order, Beethoven, Indecent Proposal,* and *The Relic.*

Fay Kanin

When I was twelve, I found out for the first time that you could get money for writing. Until then, I had always written—from one-line stories in kindergarten, to a parcel of first prizes in fourth-, fifth-, and sixth-grade essay contests. I liked words. I liked putting them together into sentences and moving them around to make them mean different things. I liked thinking that they could make someone laugh—or maybe cry. It never occurred to me that writing was for anything but the pure pleasure of doing it.

I don't know what twist of fate led me to notice the column in the *Elmira Star Gazette*. Elmira is the town in upstate New York where I spent a lot of what I like to call my formative years. It was known for housing the New York State Reformatory and Elmira College, the first educational institution to give women a degree equal to that of men. But at the moment, both were beyond me.

Maybe the column was a new Sunday feature, I don't remember, but it caught my eye, nestled between the crossword puzzle and the weekly editorial. "MY MOST EMBARRASSING MOMENT. Writers will receive a dollar each for the three best letters describing their most embarrassing moment."

I read it over several times. True, a dollar was not a princely sum, but it bought more in those days. And it was more than I had ever gotten for writing anything. I racked my brain for embarrassing moments. It wasn't hard—life, it seemed, was full of them. I picked one, wrote it and sent it off. The following week dragged by. On Sunday, I was up early to meet the paperboy at 6:30 A.M. And there it was, the first letter in the column—"MY MOST EMBARRASSING MOMENT by Fay Mitchell!"

How to describe what you feel the first time you see something you've written in newsprint? The excitement, the pride. And the next day when the dollar arrived, I fingered it appreciatively and put it away under a sweater in my bureau drawer.

Even then an idea was forming. There were more embarrassing moments and more dollars out there. Why not write another letter, but under another name? My best girlfriend (who invariably earned a C minus in English composition) loaned me hers. It appeared in the column the next week to the astonishment, I'm sure, of our English teacher.

In time, I was responsible for all three of the letters in the weekly column, under different borrowed names, of course.

Though today my sweater drawer is full of a great many more dollars, that first one, framed on the wall of my office, serves to remind me of the day I learned the ultimate validity of authorship. Being paid.

Fay Kanin was a four-term president of the Academy of Motion Picture Arts and Sciences, only one of two women who ever occupied that position in its history. She served for ten years as chair of the Foreign Language Film Executive Committee and is at present its vice-chair. A member of the Board of Trustees of the American Film Institute, she co-chairs its Center for Film and Video Preservation. She also chairs the National Film Preservation Board in Washington, mandated by Congress since 1989.

Her films have won awards in every field—an Academy Award® nomination for *Teacher's Pet,* which she co-wrote with her husband, Michael Kanin; and Emmy, Peabody, Christopher, Writers Guild awards for *Heat of Anger, Tell Me Where It Hurts, Hustling, Friendly Fire,* and *Heartsounds.* Her Broadway play, *Rashomon,* which she and her husband co-wrote, has been produced all over the world, and recently her musical, *Grind,* directed by Harold Prince, appeared on Broadway and won a Tony nomination. The Writers Guild of America, for which she served as president of the Screen Branch, honored her with its prestigious Valentine Davies and Morgan Cox awards.

LAWRENCE KASDAN

THE FIRST TIME
I HAD AN OFFICE TO WRITE IN

THE FIRST TIME I had an office to write in, it belonged to one of the greatest screenwriters of all time. Not me. This other guy.

One summer day in 1977 my agent asked me to lunch, which was so unusual it made me nervous. It had taken me a long time to get an agent, so naturally I was worried about hanging on to him. For two years now he had been trying to sell a thriller I had written for my favorite star, Steve McQueen, who didn't know I'd written this thriller for him. Originally the agent thought he wouldn't have much trouble selling my script, so he agreed to represent me. But after sixty-seven rejections, he was getting discouraged.

During that time he repeatedly suggested that, based on my screenplay, he might be able to get me work in television. *Starsky and Hutch* was the show that seemed most promising to him. But I demurred. I wanted to make movies. As I told him, I already had a job I hated—I was working in advertising—and I didn't want another one.

I was young.

When we'd settled in a booth at Hamburger Hamlet, my agent told me that he was disappointed and regretful, but since he couldn't sell my thriller, or my next script, he was going to have to drop me as a client.

I was very upset. I couldn't even finish my Henry the Fifth burger. I asked for a reprieve. I told him I was about to complete my new screenplay and that he should read it before he cut me loose. And, oh yeah, I would now consider employment on *Starsky and Hutch*. He reluctantly agreed.

A week later he called with the news that the folks at *Starsky and Hutch* had read my screenplay and didn't think I had what it took to work on the show. I told my agent I was on page 108 of my new script and he should not do anything rash. I'd call him as soon as I was done. I thought I had bought myself another week or so.

But when I came into my job the next day, there was a message that my agent had called. Could he have changed his mind overnight? Of course he could. After nine years of writing screenplays without success, I believed only bad things were going to happen.

But what he had to tell me wasn't bad. It was kind of miraculous. After two years and all that rejection, suddenly two different parties were interested in my thriller—which was called *The Bodyguard*. One interested party was an independent producer and the other was the head of production at Warner Bros., a man whose name held legendary sway for me—John Calley.

Under Calley's aegis Warners had made some of the best films of Hollywood's modern golden age: *Woodstock, Klute, Dirty*

Harry, A Clockwork Orange, McCabe and Mrs. Miller, Deliverance, Jeremiah Johnson, The Exorcist, Mean Streets, All The President's Men.

In addition, from where I was sitting (a copywriter's office in the Mutual Benefit Building at mid-Wilshire) he seemed the coolest studio executive of all time—tall, bearded, urbane, erudite, connected. Judging from the kind of publicity he got, his mind encompassed the whole business and beyond. Movies were a passion for him, but so was life. He was a yachtsman, bon vivant and genius commodities trader.

I had always hoped *The Bodyguard* would be a Warners movie. The studio that made *Bullitt* and was home to McQueen was the natural place for my story. They offered to option the script for one year. The price for the option and one rewrite was just enough, I calculated, for me to quit my job and support my family for one year of writing.

My heart raced a little as I was waved through the gate at Burbank and directed toward Calley's office. (To this day, my pulse revs every time they let me on a studio lot.) As I approached Calley's lair, which was one-half of a bungalow behind the main administration building, I saw another small building with a sign—Malpaso Productions. In front was a parking space marked "CLINT EASTWOOD—Absolutely No Parking! Don't Do It!" (It was studio legend that on more than one occasion Clint had taken a baseball bat to cars parked in his spot.)

The front entrance of Calley's bungalow was partially blocked by the back of a shiny green Rolls-Royce. When you entered the building you had a choice of two doors, the right unmarked, the left wide open. Through the open door I was hailed by Calley's secretary, an Englishwoman named Margaret, who greeted me like an old friend and settled me in a velvety sofa in the living room. The continent-size coffee table was heaped with books, scripts, art, and dozens of catalogs, the likes of which I had never seen. They must have been printed for a small audience indeed—what they were selling were mammoth, ocean-going yachts and exotic cars of the English destroyer class.

Calley hustled in from the back room wearing a sweater and open-necked shirt (British, I assumed). He greeted me warmly, flopped down opposite and immediately started asking questions about my life. His affect: confidential, focused, informal and charming. Most charming, of course, was how convincingly he went on about my talent. His enthusiasm was contagious and inclusive. He had a way of talking about "Steve" and "Barbra" and "Jack" and "Dusty" that made you feel part of the group, as though he'd be talking to them about "Larry" in his next meeting.

We talked about my rewrite. He didn't want much changed. Perhaps, he suggested, the end could leave open the possibility that the bodyguard and the singing star might meet again some day. This seemed reasonable enough to me.

He wanted me to get started right away so he could take the script to McQueen and Barbra Streisand, who he was sure would want to do it. I told him that'd be great, but I didn't think Streisand would want to do it. The character was awfully close to her persona and the story might be a little scary for her.

"Oh, she'll do it," he said. "They'll both jump on this."

Wow, I thought, this is really easy.

"Where are you going to work?" he asked.

"Well, I wanted to talk to you about that," I began, in a manner obsequiously appropriate to my station. "I was wondering if I could get an office here on the lot."

He regarded me thoughtfully. For a panicky moment I worried I had blown the deal. Not only had I been incredibly aggressive in the negotiation—I had pushed my agent to get seven thousand dollars more than they had originally offered—but now I was making unreasonable perklike demands.

"You know," Calley said, "Robert's working out at the beach. Why don't you use his office while he's gone?"

"Robert?"

"Robert Towne. I'm sure he wouldn't mind. It's just sitting there."

Robert Towne. He might just as well have said Joseph Conrad. Towne was a deity to me. He had written three of the most important movies in my life—*The Last Detail, Shampoo* and *Chinatown.* Rumor had it he'd done mysterious, important, uncredited work on *Bonnie and Clyde, The Parallax View* and *The Godfather.* He was simply the best around, the Roberto Clemente of active American screenwriters.

"Uh-huh," I said. "Where's his office?"

Calley jumped up from his English easy chair.

"It's right here! Come on."

He led me out past Margaret's desk and across the little entry hall, where he threw open the door to the other half of the bungalow, a space equal in size to Calley's own suite. It was serenely furnished with Towne's own furniture, books and art. There were at least three framed photographs of Towne's beloved dogs—giant stacks of stringy white fur called Komondors. More confirmation of my suspicion that everything in Hollywood was different from the world I knew, even the pets.

"Are you sure this is going to be all right?" I asked.

"Oh, yeah," said Calley, "Robert's great. And this way you and I can talk whenever we want. Hey, look at this."

With a big grin he turned and headed into the back of the suite. Unlike me and the people I knew in the regular world, he didn't seem worried about anything. I felt I understood the phrase "blithe spirit" for the first time.

"This whole bungalow used to be Jack Warner's private office. It was so big we divided it in two. Take a look at this bathroom."

He led me into a space the size of my own living room in Sherman Oaks. It had been intricately decorated with Italian tiles and special lighting. There was a cavernous sauna and a bathtub that could hold six adults (and probably had).

Margaret called from the front room.

"John, I have Kubrick calling from London. Do you want him?"

Calley made a face.

"I'd better see what he wants. Why don't you look around? See if this'll work for you."

Suddenly he was gone, and I was alone. In Robert Towne's office. In Jack Warner's bathroom. I noticed for the first time that one entire wall was mirrored. But not just mirrored. The glass had been tinted a delicate amber, so that anyone reflected in it seemed to have a perfect tan.

I regarded my own image. It seemed to me that I had never looked so good.

Lawrence Kasdan has written or co-written twelve films and directed nine, including the forthcoming *Mumford*. He has been nominated for six Writers Guild Awards (winning for *The Big Chill*), four Academy Awards®, and a Directors Guild Award.

NICHOLAS KAZAN

MY LIFE as a writer began in the theater. The first time I wrote a real play, I was in college, eating breakfast, and heard a single line of dialogue echoing over and over in my mind. Intrigued, I moved to the typewriter (yes, it was that long ago) and took dictation (there's no other word for it) for two straight hours during which the characters, their plight, and every aspect of the drama was thrown at me at blazing speed without a moment of hesitation, doubt, or contemplative thought. The play (a one-act) was produced in college, produced professionally, and hardly a line changed from that first astounding burst.

This was, I hardly need add, definitely *not* an experience which prepared me for Hollywood (no rewrites?!), but it remains the most important two hours of my life, because it changed me, made me a writer for good (or bad) and forever, and I still come to my computer every day in the hope that I will have that ecstatic experience of being a slave to forces, voices, visions beyond my ken. It does still happen: not as frequently as I'd like, but often enough to keep me pleasantly enslaved.

The first job I had in Hollywood was, I later found out, a cost-of-doing-business expense for Universal Studios which wanted to keep a Legendary Figure happy by developing (at virtually no expense, I got scale) a script of his "dream" (read "fantasy" read "never-will-be-made") project. "Are you a visual scenarist?" the Legendary Figure asked me. I figured there could only be one correct answer to that question, got the answer right, got the job, got paid, wasted my time.

Two years later, reflecting on this experience, I decided the Legendary Figure might have been onto something. Maybe it wasn't a bad idea to actually *be* a visual scenarist. I wrote a script with almost no dialogue. The result was startling. For the first time, I realized, I was writing *film*.

The first time I sold a script (yes, the one without much dialogue), I had the temerity to insist that, before the deal was closed, I meet the "Creative" Executive to find out what the studio wanted in the way of revisions. Creative Exec's concerns seemed minor, his enthusiasm genuine; I was sold. Down the river, it turns out. After the deal was agreed upon, Creative Exec and I had a second meeting where his *real* notes emerged. I left the room in a state of shock. Called my lawyer. "We don't have a signed deal yet, do we?"

"No," he said.

"And money hasn't changed hands?"

"No."

"So our deal so far is just *verbal*, right?"

"Right."

"And is based on their *verbal* assurances that the upcoming script work is minor, right?"

At this point, my lawyer grew uncharacteristically silent.

"Well," I said, "it turns out those verbal assurances were fraudulent, so the verbal deal is off."

My lawyer—and agent I might add—were somewhat startled to have a client attempting to extricate himself from his First Real Opportunity in the Business, but they did their duty.

They called the studio.

An hour later, the Creative Exec called back. I have always considered his response to be a perfect example of good writing: powerful, succinct, and freighted with subtext: "We have a very large legal staff."

Being a relative novice in entertainment law and lacking an advanced degree in semiology, I did not immediately decode this statement. "What does it mean?" I asked my lawyer.

"It means they want your script, and if you try to void the agreement, they'll tie you up in court forever, so that all you'll see from the script are my legal bills. And no other company will dare touch the script when it's clouded by this studio's prior claim, however bogus that claim may be."

"Oh."

I took their money.

I rewrote the script per their suggestions, which were as bad as any I would ever receive (despite, as you might imagine, some pretty determined competition during the years that followed).

I turned in my rewrite and was quickly replaced, rewritten, forgotten. By some odd quirk of fate, the film was actually made.

I saw a rough cut and asked to use a pseudonym. (Yes, I actually decided to forgo my very first shared credit.) The studio was kind enough to comply, but they weren't done with me. Not only did they not dislike my script, they also disliked my pseudonym. They rewrote it without my permission. There's a lesson in there somewhere, and I suspect it's not that heavily buried, but I am loath to lift the rock and find out what it looks like.

The first time I said no (as in "No, I will not do that to my script"), it was a liberating experience. In all honesty, I don't remember the exact occasion, but I know for sure it was liberating because it's *always* liberating: every single time, no matter how weak or powerful one may be, no matter how many times one has said it before, no matter how much—or little—one is risking.

"No" is the single most important thing a writer can say. It must be said politely, often obliquely ("I'll think about it" or "Can I go to the bathroom now?"), but with great frequency. It must usually, for the sake of politeness, be explained by citing dire consequences. (To the film, I mean, not to the physical well-being of the Powers That Be.) To be honest, explaining seldom does any good at the time, but sometimes said Powers actually *remember* what you said and rehire you later to repair the damage done in your absence.

"No" sometimes means you are quitting the project, which is often the only way to avoid murdering your own child. At other times, "no" results in your dismissal, and that's okay too. Ultimately all we have are our visions and our voices: They feed our minds, they *are* our talent, and we must protect them fiercely, at all costs.

––––––––––

Nicholas Kazan is the author of thirty unproduced screenplays and eleven movies that have been made.

RICHARD LAGRAVANESE

THE FIRST TIME I wrote for the sake of writing was in fourth grade when I was nine. We had this rule in class that if you finished your work, you could get a book and read it until everyone was finished. Having read all the books, I decided to write a short story. It was called "James Bond and the Girl with the Buck Teeth" and it was all about Bond being given a female partner who wasn't beautiful and then winds up falling in love with her. It strikes me, remembering this incident, that I have been writing the same story ever since. My teacher gave me an A for extra credit.

The first time I felt acknowledged as a writer was in acting class. I started writing monologues for myself and fellow acting students, because I got tired of auditioning with Biff from *Death of a Salesman* or Richard from *Ah, Wilderness!* My first monologue was about my father. He was a cab driver in New York and

I described the time he picked up Marilyn Monroe and had her sit in the front seat. Other students started asking me for monologues and, for a small fee, I provided them.

The first time one of them was performed (by my best friend) it went over very well. Her performance was fantastic. My acting teacher then turned to me and said, quite simply, "And the writing is good." For some reason, that acknowledgment meant a great deal to me.

That same teacher submitted my name to Joan Micklin Silver who was putting together an Off-Broadway revue about women called *A . . . My Name Is Alice*. She was collecting material, i.e., songs, scenes, monologues. I gave her the same monologue my friend performed and it was accepted. The first writing I ever sold. It was a monologue about a woman doing the laundry and having a conversation with her unfaithful lover, imagining him in the dryer trapped in his own jockstrap. I did my first rewrite one Saturday morning when Joan called at 11 A.M. I had only gone to bed at 8 A.M. This was the early eighties in New York—a period we lovingly refer to as Ancient Rome. But there was an ease I felt in the process. The rewrite took fifteen minutes. It's never been that easy since. Returning to that state of blissful unknowing knowing—creating out of an intuition, ignorant of success or failure—is an ongoing goal. The moments that I can recapture that are invaluable.

The first time I received steady pay for writing was during the period I was working a survival job at the Metropolitan Opera House selling tickets. For extra money, I wrote phone sex monologues for High Society. The rules were: No vulgar language, only euphemisms . . . and every monologue had to end with an orgasm. I gave titles to mine, even though the only person who would see the title would be the girl recording the monologue. But it gave me a satisfying, albeit ridiculous, sense of authorship . . . "At the Movies" . . . "In the Love Canal" . . . "The Meter Is Running" . . .

I think another significant first would be the first time I hit THE WALL . . . You know THE WALL? That point when you're in the screenplay, you're moving along steadily, you're writing great scenes, great moments, great dialogue—and then it suddenly occurs to you that none of it works as a whole. It's as if you've been making a suit of clothes and suddenly notice a piece of string hanging off the jacket, so you decide to pull it, causing both sleeves and all the buttons to fall off. It happened while I was writing *The Fisher King*. I didn't know what I was doing. I had written three previous drafts with completely different stories but the same two main characters. I finally came upon Jack being a radio talk-show personality. But I couldn't figure out how to get Jack and the character of Parry to interconnect. I was lying on the couch, paralyzed. I'd written scenes, I knew what I wanted to say, I knew where I wanted to go thematically but damn—where was the frigging plot? I was so lost I stared at the same point on the ceiling for about three hours. My life passed before me, including the future—a future filled with misery, poverty and loneliness. Yes, that's what arriving at THE WALL feels like. So, I gave up.

And then, a little idea filtered in. Something about responsibility. About cause and effect. Something about Jack's blind ambition for laughter and success affecting a fan with a weak mind. And how that humiliated man creates a violent situation that affects Parry's life forever. And so, Jack became connected to Parry through the idea of having Parry's wife killed in the restaurant by the man Jack irresponsibly influenced, affected, used on the radio . . . After that, the script wrote itself.

First times are important. And somehow, we have to maintain the spirit of those experiences, no matter how many years or how much experience separates us from them. Every time I begin a screenplay, I feel like I'm flying without a net and I don't know a damn thing. It's the mystery of imagination. You can never know how it works. You can only create a relationship to it, have faith and be bold enough to "lose sight of the shore" every now and then in order "to discover new lands."

––––––––––

Richard LaGravanese is the screenwriter of *The Fisher King, The Ref, The Little Princess, The Bridges of Madison County, Unstrung Heroes, The Mirror Has Two Faces, The Horse Whisperer,* and writer/director of *Living Out Loud.*

PETER LEFCOURT

THE FIRST TIME I got paid for it was very nearly the last time. It was that weird. Here's what happened. The names have been changed because several of the principals are still operating heavy machinery.

Circa 1974. I was a youngish writer out from the East with about $800 of fuck-you money in my pocket. I was living in a $140-a-month apartment in Venice and driving a 1957 VW with serious transmission problems. If you do the math you can see that I was a couple of months away from a busboy's job at Denny's.

I did, however, have an agent. And I use that term loosely. I happen to know that this guy is, in fact, still operating heavy machinery because he calls me regularly to pitch clients. The sum total of this agent's advice in the months we had allegedly been in business together was, "write TV movies, kid." I dutifully wrote TV movies. Women-in-jeopardy movies—wom-jeps, or Cloris-

Leachman-in-jeopardy movies as they were called in the vernac-
ular—were in vogue at the moment. I tossed off a few wom-jeps,
which my putative agent pronounced too soft and that was that.
Denny's beckoned.

One foggy day in April, with Denny's less than a month away,
I received a phone call from my putative agent's putative assistant.

"You got a meeting at Paramount tomorrow at 2:30."

"I do? With whom?"

He mentioned a name I had never heard, the producer of a
TV cop series I had never watched.

"They'll leave a drive-on pass for you at the Windsor Gate."
To give you an idea just how well things had been going for me I
did not tell my putative agent's putative assistant that I had never
seen this show and had no idea what to pitch. No. This was an actual meeting, presumably with a person who could arrange to
have a check cut. So I went across the hall and asked my neighbor, a man who wrote sadomasochistic porn novels, if he had
ever watched this show.

"Never miss it," he said and then proceeded to give me a
quick overview of the characters and basic premise.

I drove to Paramount the next day with a half dozen stories in
my gun. There was no drive-on pass waiting for me at the
Windsor Gate. I explained I was a writer for this show, and, after
a phone call back to the office, I was admitted.

As soon as I walked into the office suite, I sensed that there
was something wiggy going on. There were phones ringing behind closed doors, hushed conversations, a pervasive sense of
anxiety in the air. I was parked in the corner, given a cup of coffee
and ignored for an hour.

Finally, the producer of this TV series emerged from behind his closed door and, offering no apology for the hour wait, ushered me into a very dark office with mahogany furniture, a dartboard, and framed pictures of the producer deep-sea fishing off Baja. When he told me how much he admired my work, I knew why there had been no pass waiting for me at the Windsor Gate.

But I was in his office, armed with stories. There seemed to be no point in clearing up the misunderstanding.

So I pitched. Badly. After all, I had never done this before, and as the Deep-Sea Fisherman threw darts at his dartboard, I went on and on with a great deal of extraneous detail. After maybe ten minutes, he said, "I don't hear any lights and sirens . . ."

I started to back and fill, as best I could—not yet the master of the middle-of-the-meeting back and fill—when the phone rang. He listened for a long time and then said, "shit." He said "shit" several times before hanging up.

Without saying anything else to me, he made several phone calls, one after another, until his door opened and an unkempt but friendly-looking man with a full beard entered. With the Deep-Sea Fisherman still on the phone, the bearded man beckoned me to follow him out of the office.

We waded back through the pent-up anxiety to another, much smaller, office. The man, who looked like a Russian anarchist, introduced himself as the story editor and asked me if I had any plans for the weekend.

"No" was apparently the right answer because ten minutes later I was employed for a story/option teleplay for a 60-minute prime-time TV episode, about $3,800 at the time. This was more money than I had ever seen at one time, and I congratulated myself that I had apparently dodged Denny's for at least six more months.

The story editor asked me to repeat my story ideas. He gri-maced, frowned and finally selected one which he said was not completely *fercocta*. I had not yet learned the argot of the busi-ness, but I assumed, correctly, that "not being completely *fer-cocta*" was a good thing.

For the next eight hours I got a crash course in story con-struction from a man who had been doing it for many years. By 11 that night we had the story broken, and I was permitted to go home for a few hours sleep on the condition that I report back to Paramount at 9 A.M. sharp the next day.

On that Saturday, deserted by both the Deep-Sea Fisherman and the Russian Anarchist and guarded only by a typist in the otherwise empty outer office, I wrote Act I of Episode 13 of the cop show in a tiny office with nothing but a desk and an IBM Selectric. On Sunday I wrote Act II. When I was finished with a scene I would give the pages to the typist. The phone rang three times all weekend. It was the Russian Anarchist with breezy en-couragement. "You're doing a great job. Don't stop."

On Monday morning I was on to Act III. The office suite was once again populated, but the anxiety that had been more or less subliminal on Friday was right out in the open. People were put-ting their personal belongings into boxes. The Deep-Sea Fisher-man was nowhere to be found, but the Russian Anarchist was in his office, putting his things in boxes.

"The show's been canceled," he informed me cheerfully.

When he saw the look of panic in my eyes he quickly reas-sured me that I would be paid for my script. Not only would I be paid but the script would be shot. In fact, it was being shot as we spoke, and I had better get back to my office and get those pages out. They had five and a half days to shoot the entire episode and they were already on Day 1. And, by the way, lose the exterior driving shot of the cop car. Make it an interior in the lieutenant's office. They had the standing set.

I asked the Russian Anarchist when they found out that the show had gone south and he told me they had known Friday. "We thought the considerate thing to do was not to tell you. It would have been distracting." I thanked him for his consideration.

So all that week I sat in a tiny office at Paramount and wrote a script for a canceled cop show that was being shot as I wrote it. I got no notes except from the line producer, who would call me from the set and tell me to move something inside, to remove a character, to shorten a scene, to make night day or day night.

By the time I was finished accommodating the production, the story made absolutely no sense whatsoever. Not that it had ever made a lot of sense to begin with. I never saw either the Deep-Sea Fisherman or the Russian Anarchist again. There was no wrap party for this show. The last one out the door must have shut down the camera.

Fortunately for everyone involved, the episode never aired. It was just the completion of the network's production commitment to the studio, or vice versa—essentially an accounting decision to amortize the costs over 13 episodes instead of 12 while the damage control dance of closing down a canceled show went on.

When I called my putative agent, who actually took my call now that I was generating income, he apologized for the whole mess. Actually he had wanted to call _____, a successful writer whose name was right before mine in the Rolodex, and his putative assistant had dialed mine by mistake.

"Fucking kick in the head, huh? But, hey, all's well that ends well, right?"

"Right."

"Write TV movies, kid," he said and hung up.

The episode is presumably locked away in a vault somewhere at Paramount. I have an occasional nightmare that someone is going to dig up this piece of film and make me watch it. Either that, or send me to Denny's for a week of hard labor.

———

Peter Lefcourt is the author of five eclectically disreputable novels: *The Deal, The Dreyfus Affair, Di and I, Abbreviating Ernie,* and *The Woody.* His day job is writing and producing film and television. He's currently the co-creator/executive producer of the darkly irreverent Showtime satire *Beggars and Choosers.*

CHUCK LORRE

THE FIRST TIME I GOT FIRED

OF ALL THE TIMES I've been fired, I guess the first will always seem just a little special. In later years I would have my run-ins with Roseanne, Brett Butler and Cybill Shepherd, but only one of them would actually fire me (the other two I would leave of my own volition, shortly after I had what were later described to me as "classic nervous breakdowns"). Which is why it was my ouster as head writer and executive producer of *Beany & Cecil* that still stands out as a sweet, noble memory.

In the spring of 1988 ABC approached me to write and produce a remake of the old Bob Clampett cartoon. Having only recently crawled into a story editor position on the sitcom *My Two Dads,* and being filled with the natural hubris that accompanies such an exalted status, the idea of working on some insipid Saturday morning cartoon was laughable. I politely declined.

Then the Writers Guild strike hit, grinding all live-action, prime-time shows to a complete halt. I was suddenly out of work and facing a mountain of monthly bills that only a story editor with executive story editor expectations could accumulate. I quickly called ABC back and told them I had reconsidered. For good measure I said *Beany* was a rare jewel of family entertainment, and that I would be deeply honored to write and produce it. To my great relief, they hired me anyway. I felt pretty darn smug. Little did I know that dark forces were already conspiring against me.

Part of my deal was that I would be working with the son of the late Bob Clampett. It seemed Junior had spent several years struggling to capture his father's vision to ABC's satisfaction, and had come up empty-handed. He was none too happy when I arrived, booted up my trusty Wordstar program and quickly generated the script and show bible that would green-light the series for a fall launch. I was oblivious to his pain. Something for which I would later pay dearly.

The devastating strike wore on, but I was now fully, and quite legitimately, employed (writing for animation was not covered by Guild rules). In fact, times were good. Instead of financial ruin, I had actually doubled my income. Many of television's best writers, desperate to pay their West Side condo mortgages and West Valley alimonies, were calling me for work. Highly respected scribes, who only weeks before were writing for Steven Bochco, were now dreaming up ways in which Dishonest John could bamboozle that lovable sea serpent, Cecil. Nyah-ha-ha!

But the good times were not to last. A talented young animator (who would later go on to create *Ren & Stimpy*) was added to our creative team. He had his own ideas for the show—ideas which would one day work brilliantly on *Ren & Stimpy*. We had creative differences.

Try as I might, I could not stand by and let good ol' Ceec puke up his own eyeballs, or step inside a giant conch shell to (wink, wink) "pleasure himself." It just didn't seem true to the spirit of the show.

I suddenly found myself in the unlikely position of having to defend the artistic integrity of "Beany & freaking Cecil." I was emotional. I was passionate. I was filled with self-righteousness. Why I gave a shit is a mystery I've yet to unravel.

Anyway, things heated up quickly. Junior saw his chance to regain the throne and joined forces with the Walt Disney of toilet, onanism, and vomit jokes. A formidable power bloc was now allied against me. Every script I turned in was rewritten without my permission. The production process was completely shut down. I screamed my outrage to the network and production company. Lines were drawn, sides were chosen. The widow Clampett (possibly the prototype for Cecil's antagonist) joined forces with her son, thinking perhaps that his genes carried the seed of greatness she had once loved.

The final showdown took place in an ominously lit corporate boardroom dominated by a long, expensive, mahogany table. The room smelled of syndication profits and all the limited-animation honchos were there. I dimly noticed that everyone—the network and production company execs, the Clampetts and Stimpy's dad—were sitting on one side of the table . . . facing me. I say "dimly" because I had yet to realize the precariousness of my situation.

Young Clampett got quickly to the point and angrily accused me of ruining the show. I lost it. At that moment I became so enraged, I literally saw red. When my vision returned, I replied that if it weren't for me, my accuser would be working at a Taco Bell, asking customers if they wanted lids on their shakes.

Widow Clampett reacted with a mother's fury. She leapt to her feet yelling that I couldn't talk to her son that way. I said I'd talk to the little knucklehead anyway I wanted and he was old enough to stop hiding behind his mommy's apron.

Eventually the designated grown-ups in the room restored order and the meeting was adjourned. But here's the really funny part: When I found out the following day that I'd been fired, I was surprised. Didn't they know? Didn't they understand? I was fighting the good fight! I was keeping *Beany & Cecil* pure for a whole new generation! I was fucking nuts, is what I was. Which was when I learned one of the basic axioms of show business: The people who own the project, or in some cases the people who *are* the project, have the inalienable right to destroy the project. Which is exactly what happened. The series was revamped by my adversaries, Cecil began farting sea anemones, hilarity didn't ensue, and the show was quickly canceled.

Well there it is, the first time I got fired . . . as a writer. For the record, I'd previously been terminated as a busboy (I adamantly refused to clean up the women's washroom after something odd happened in it); a pharmacy clerk (the pharmacist overheard me telling a customer to "ease up on the quaaludes, dude"); a window washer (that was my fault, I had trouble showing up for work at 4 A.M.); a guitarist in a Samoan lounge band (creative differences); a guitarist in a Spike Jones cover band (also creative differences); and finally, as a husband (I'd love to chalk that one up to creative differences as well, but I have it on pretty good authority that I was just an asshole).

———————

Chuck Lorre is a New York native who considers himself to be the luckiest guitar player in America. He feels certain that had he not stumbled into television, he'd still be doing four sets a night at Big Daddy's Lounge in Long Beach and sleeping on some unfortunate woman's couch.

NAT MAULDIN

THE FIRST TIME I got paid was for an obituary. It was 1977, and I had no idea what I wanted to do with my life. I majored in art before dropping out of college, went to acting school, drove a shuttle van, worked at a PR firm and an animation studio. Nothing felt right. During the summer I moved to New York and landed a job as one of the voices on *SportsLine*, a pre–information highway dial-in service that offered fans up-to-the-minute scores recorded on a loop several times each hour. I was hired principally because of my ability to recite an entire day's worth of them (NBA, NHL and NFL on weekends) in 59 seconds or less.

We received hundreds of thousands of calls each week (mostly, I still believe, from bookmakers and shut-ins) prompting our ambitious parent company to launch an entire string of *Lines*, delivering information and advice on everything from traffic to astrology. In October, they introduced one called *MusicLine*. Its voice, an alcoholic ex-deejay from Connecticut, had long since stumbled off to Grand Central one night when word came in on the AP wire that a Convair turboprop carrying the rock group Lynyrd Skynyrd had just gone down in a Mississippi swamp, and that its lead singer Ronnie VanZant had been one of those killed.

Our parent company quickly powwowed on a conference call. They believed that immediacy was the element that set our *Lines* apart (from what, I'm not sure), and decided this was *MusicLine*'s big chance for legitimacy. Surely people would hear about the crash, lunge for their phones and call for details. If they heard them, if they were informed and even consoled on the very same night it happened, then we were for real. Being the only voice left in the studio, I was pressed into service to write and record a *MusicLine* "Special Edition" on the spot.

As my musical tastes tended to lean toward Motown and oldies, I had no idea who Ronnie VanZant was. Still, the Lynyrd Skynyrd hit "Sweet Home Alabama" was one of those songs that radio stations enjoyed clubbing you over the head with, so I was aware of who they were . . . sort of. It was a new band, right? (Played together since junior high.) And they were from Alabama, of course. (Florida.) Clearly my familiarity with all things Skynyrd would give me the tools necessary to come up with something that would be both enlightening and poignant.

I wrote it on a legal pad and delivered it in the requisite 59 seconds. I vaguely remember passages like "the tragedy of losing an artist who was so young and vital," "the raw honesty in his voice," and, alluding to the Iowa plane crash that killed Buddy Holly, lamenting how places like swamps and wheat

fields were such terrible, lonely places to die. Something like
that.

I waited for the scores from the West Coast to come in, put
SportsLine to bed, forgot about it and went home. The next day
the phone calls started early. "What an amazing job." "I was moved
to tears." "Who knew you were a VanZant aficionado?" At the
office, two secretaries came out of their cubicles to congratulate
me, one at each end of the hall. I couldn't believe it. It was so easy.

The following Friday there were two checks in my envelope.
The one I got every week, and another one marked "Creative
Services." $200 for fifteen minutes of work. I didn't even know the
guy. Surely this was as close as I would ever come to receiving a
sign from above. It was like the scene where Roy Hobbs got his
first bat . . . a bolt of lightning struck the hapless little tree outside
my apartment window on 23rd Street, and when the smoke
cleared, there, sitting on the curb, was a smoldering IBM
Selectric.

Within a year, *MusicLine* had folded, the parent company had
filed for Chapter 11, and I had sold my first sitcom script and was
headed out west in a used Toyota. Somewhere around Kansas a
rock station happened to play another Skynyrd song, which I
cranked. It was the live version of "Free Bird" they had recorded
for their fourth album (they have since released a dozen more),
and it was only then that I realized just how good these guys
were, especially VanZant. The rest of my obit might've been hollow crap, but damned if there wasn't a raw honesty in his voice.

I smiled. Here I was on my way to Hollywood—surely the
things I'd be paid for writing out there would be more genuine,
more honorable—and the raw, honest and forgiving spirit of
Ronnie himself was serenading me down the road:

"'Cause I'm as free as a bird now, And this bird you cannot change, Lord help me, I can't change."

———————

Nat Mauldin joined the Writers Guild in 1978. He has written scripts for such TV shows as *Barney Miller, Newhart, Night Court,* and *Have Faith,* and the screenplays for *Downtown, The Preacher's Wife,* and *Dr. Dolittle.* He won a WGA Award in 1983 in the Best Episodic Comedy category. He lives with his wife and two children in Los Angeles.

PETER MEHLMAN

THE FIRST TIME I got paid to write, I was 21 and had mononucleosis. I couldn't play basketball, I couldn't date. All I could do was read and write. When you get right down to it, mononucleosis launched my career.

At the time, I just graduated from the University of Maryland and settled into that classic postcollegiate stage known as stupidity. Having no idea what I'd do with my life, mononucleosis was a calming option. For six weeks, I was under doctor's orders not to do anything with my life. So I sat by the pool in my apartment complex and read seven books by Philip Roth. Just as I was polishing off *My Life as a Man*, a summer school student came over and asked if I ever read anything by anyone else other than Philip Roth. I said no. In a Non-Sequiturs-R-Us way, he said he had a copy aide job at the *Washington Post*.

"That sounds good," I said.

"Forget it," he shot back, "they're not hiring any more white males. Washington is 83 percent black. They can't hire any more whites."

That night, a girl I knew from school dropped over to see how I was doing. She had no idea what to do with her life either, so, in lieu of mono, she decided to get a deep tan, wear a jumpsuit unzipped down to the cleavage sphere, and visit a 21-year-old with mono.

"Don't get too close," she whispered, "I don't want to get sick."

I nudged her to leave, jumped to my typewriter and furiously wrote an insane but funny job letter to the *Washington Post* sports editor, posing as a woman named Faith Kates. I figured very few women applied for jobs in sports. I finished the letter at three A.M., mailed it at eight, then called my hematologist asking if mono had any detrimental effects on mental functions.

"Not according to the latest research," she said.

After a week, I was relieved to have heard nothing from the *Post.* Then while diving into *The Professor of Desire,* I got a note from George Solomon, the sports editor of the *Washington Post.* "Dear Faith . . ." it began.

Having enjoyed my letter, he offered me a copy aide job with "lousy hours—eight P.M. to two A.M. with Mondays and Tuesdays off."

I wrote a letter back, explaining that my name was not Faith and I wasn't a woman and I'm terribly sorry for writing a job letter in drag.

In the middle of "Our Gang," I got another letter on *Washington Post* stationery. "Dear Peter/Faith . . ." it began.

I was invited up to the newsroom.

George Solomon was a short, pudgy, sharp-witted man who

spoke in clipped sentences uttered within three inches of your face. He spoke to me at such close range, I imagined him a substitute point guard making up for his lack of height by feverishly boxing me out for rebounds. I told him I was just getting over mononucleosis. He didn't back off an inch. Instead, he called over other editors to meet "the kid who wrote the funny letter as a girl." One editor said to me, "You know, you write a little like Philip Roth."

As Ben Bradlee, Bob Woodward and Sally Quinn crossed the newsroom from the Style Section to Metro, I said, "Well, I like to write . . ."

Solomon stepped back, thought for a second, then jumped back into my airspace. "Tell you what, Mehlman." (He's calling me Mehlman. It's like I'm on staff already.) "How would you like to do a little feature story?" (A feature. Yes, I could do a feature. I like features.) "There are a bunch of guys who hang out over the rail everyday at Laurel Raceway. They're called 'railbirds.'" (Railbirds. Yes, that makes sense. They hang over the rail like birds.) "Do a little scene piece on railbirds. Eight hundred words. (Eight hundred. That's not many words. I know eight hundred words.) "Fifty bucks. That's what we'll pay you. Fifty bucks." (They're paying me?) "And don't pretend you're a girl anymore. It worked once. Don't do it again."

I went to Laurel Raceway for five days to write eight hundred words. Between admission, losing bets and lunches, I spent over ninety dollars without ever thinking of putting in for expenses. I turned in 803 words, thinking no one would notice.

Solomon read the story right in front of me. Without a trace of a smile, he said, "Funny, very funny. Good stuff. Fifty bucks. That's what you'll get. Fifty bucks."

Two weeks later, I went to a store to Xerox some copies of the check. The clerk insisted on stamping the word "COPY" on the copies so I wouldn't try to cash them. I sent a COPY of the check with a tear sheet of the article to everyone I knew.

When mononucleosis was finally gone, I started reading *When She Was Good* in the press box before a high school football game I was covering for the *Washington Post*.

Peter Mehlman is best known for his work on *Seinfeld*. After writing the series' first freelance episode, *The Apartment*, he was hired for the first full season as a program consultant (1991–1992) and, over the next six years, worked his way up to co-executive producer. He is perhaps most famous for his "Yada Yada" episode, and he is also the author of such now classic Seinfeldisms as "spongeworthy" and "shrinkage." In 1997, Mehlman joined DreamWorks and created *It's Like, You Know . . .*, a scathing and incisive look at life in the city of Los Angeles.

MARILYN SUZANNE MILLER

THERE WAS a first "First Time I Got Paid for It" and a second "First Time I Got Paid for It"; the first "First Time" was distinctive as I had never done anything for money before. I had, in fact, at 22, *had* no money, except that given me by my parents and earned in a chain store at $1.60 an hour. This first "First Time" is also distinguished for its extreme fairy-tale quality: In 1972, just out of college, facing a large bill for grad school (if I went, for an M.F.A. in writing at the University of Iowa), I called Jim Brooks, out of the blue, a cold call to the man whose name I'd seen as co-executive producer of *The Mary Tyler Moore Show*. I phoned from my parents' house in Monroeville, Pennsylvania. For reasons unknown to Jim or me even today, he took my call and I said, "Hi, I'm Marilyn Miller from Monroeville, Pennsylvania, and I have a *Mary Tyler Moore* script, will you read it?" and he said, "Yes. Please send it to me right away." (Not the presumed way such a scene should play. This was the serendipity, no doubt, of two romantics meeting on the phone.) And in this Lana-Turner-being-discovered-at-Schwab's way, two weeks later I got a partial scholarship to grad school, and a letter from James L. Brooks saying I wrote better than 70 percent of the writers out there, and that, with my permission, he would like to submit my script to every single friend he had in show business. The outsize qualities of this story, of Jim's incredible kindness, bold-faced benevolence and the follow-up miracle—that Garry Marshall flew me to L.A. where both he and Jim instantly gave me work—reduce any normal "First Time" stories to sagas of angst, delay, forestalled gratification, even grief. That God, via Jim Brooks, had intervened for me, and that I worked steadily from that day to this are the two unrivaled blessings of my very blessed life.

The second "First Time I Got Paid for It" was for a show that barely existed, and which itself *had* no money, but for which I threw over wildly lucrative offers, to work under contracts of 3 (three)-week intervals (the additional deal here: the whole show itself could be canceled, also after stints of three weeks). This stunning leap of business blind faith, I made into the arms of Lorne Michaels, to write for the brand-new *Saturday Night Live*. At 25, with three years of (principally) situation comedy under my belt, and just enough to pay my Saks bill with, I was a seasoned, high-priced veteran on this show. No one there had done *anything* for money before, except hope. Herb Sargent and I were getting "top of the show" ($750 a week, for three weeks) and it was the happiest time of my life. I had blithely joined my peers in the cogent overthrow of network television (1960s holdovers we were, raised on TV, and determined to reclaim its vision for our own).

When I first arrived, there was very little: floors, but notably, no walls. I thereby stunned John Belushi, Tom Schiller and whoever else was around with the sound of someone who knew how to type 80 words a minute. After typing my first page or two (to what I didn't realize was an awed hush) I was editing quietly when I was suddenly overwhelmed by the explosions of four typewriters doing an "impression" of me typing. Belushi, Schiller, etc., all were pretending to type at about two hundred words a minute, and would do so whenever I finished a page. I was the first actual person they ever met who could type.

There were not many secretaries, and we all answered whatever phone was ringing. Then, not knowing how to use hold buttons, screamed out, "Gilda, it's for you!" Walls did go up slowly, but phones still got answered by passersby, only now someone would yell out, "Billy, there's a call for you *in your room*," like in some Rockefeller Center–located suburban house, where some of us had our own rooms, and some (mostly actors) had to report to a sofa, in some particular corner. Doing a live 90-minute "Special" once a week, I knew to be humanly impossible, and confided such solely to Lorne, knowing he wouldn't want it to get around. Still, we did it—worked those twenty-four-hour days with pit stops for sleep, many months in a row, with the energy to spare only available to the young and insane. For example, one night while working till six A.M., Alan Zweibel and I, bored (BORED!?!), decided it would be really funny to torture the apprentice writers on the staff (Al Franken and Tom Davis) by carrying all their furniture, desks, files and everything from their office (a hall) into Herb Sargent's office (where it had to be laid endwise and crammed in: we even ripped the phones out of the floor), then leave a simple, prosaic piece of white paper on the

floor on which we had written, "See me. Lorne." With their pre-
carious jobs, somehow we thought they'd find this just a riot
(Herb, too) but, hey, you know the hours we kept; we were sometimes severely judgment challenged.

I remember, watching Herb's impassive face as he opened the
door to his office around ten A.M., wondering if it were possible
he just might, by chance, *mind* not being able to get into his
office, or to his desk forever. The reaction? Let's just say Herb was
less troubled than F. and D.

The "living together" aspect of office life was both a powerful
emollient to creativity and a roiling agony to the survival of self.
Michael O'Donoughue, in an act of craven selfhood, actually
locked his office (he had a door). Hyper organized, a practitioner
of perfect block-letter writing, a thumber-thru of index cards
and keeper of lists, Michael's bulletin boards and wall surfaces
had exactly placed cartoons, drawings, reminders and phone
numbers, in pristine configurations. Rosie Schuster got his key
from Security every night, and with sure insight into the madness of discreet organization, she moved, in exact form, shape
and relative distance, the entire display of things on Michael's
walls, each night, one inch to the right. Soon, then, phone lists
crossed the frames of his bulletin boards onto the walls—it took
weeks for Michael to realize everything he had mounted was
slowly moving as a unit around his office.

While I was not paid specifically for the experience of "The
First Time I Lived in an Office with 50 Other People," it felt like I
was. That life (including a "working Seder" on the seventeenth
floor of NBC the second season of *SNL*) showed me how expo-
nentially funnier we each grew, for being endlessly rubbed up
against each other in our open work space. No sleek corporate

doors, with their chic handles and swank latches could have stood astern a prouder, more joyfully rendered product, nor closed behind them a more loving, close if unorthodox family of peers who produced it.

These years also provided "The First Time I Went up Against the Network Censor" (and the last time: networks no longer have censors). I wrote very little censor-sensitive material, but I knew, from the guys, the gambit of getting what you want on the air: by stuffing the sketch with objectionable material you didn't really want in the sketch anyway, then finally "compromising" on the originally intended sketch. I used this method only once, in a sketch where Gilda Radner and Jane Curtin play young women who compete with each other for who got the best buy on a silk blouse, whose brother was in a better position to get her free samples, and whose menstrual period was worse (mostly that). The variegations on bad periods were so bountiful I realized I could dance through the worlds of cramps, bloating, bad skin and heavy flow, equally glib in all areas, *and* with material to trade off to the censors, with whom I ended up on the phone Saturday afternoon (the censor vice president, calling from home). This "Head Censor of All New Jersey" informed me that he didn't care if it was sexist to say this (my previous argument to him) but the part about the bad skin and heavy flow made him sick (as they did me, who nonetheless continued accusing him of being hellishly antiwomen and NBC itself of being a big sexist pig network, the last such holdout in the late twentieth century). When the censor finally *admitted* to being a big sexist pig, and said he didn't care, that stuff had to go, I knew I'd get to keep the *actual* funny parts (cramps, bloating) which were in fact the only things in the original draft at the table reading. This taught me an effective lifelong lesson: If you want cramps and bloating, *always* ask for bad skin and heavy flow, too.

All writers live through an inestimable number of "First Times," as each piece of writing is always a first. I'm glad these were some of mine.

Marilyn Suzanne Miller has written for many shows including *Saturday Night Live, The Mary Tyler Moore Show, The Tracey Ullman Show,* and *Murphy Brown.* She is the woman with the most prizes in writing in television, including three Emmys and one Humanitas Prize. Her work has appeared on the Op-Ed page of the *New York Times* and at the New York Shakespeare Festival.

DARYL G. NICKENS

THE GREAT ESCAPE—OR THE FIRST TIME I DIDN'T PAY FOR IT

THE FIRST TIME I snuck into a movie theater was the summer after my grandfather was killed. As a young man, he had been a Pullman porter, a prestigious and lucrative job in the segregated world of that time—so much so that it was not unheard of for black men with professional degrees to prefer it to the struggles of practicing their erstwhile professions; but upon marriage to my grandmother, my grandfather settled into the quiescent drudgery typically available to black men of his generation: He shined shoes, dug ditches, slung hash—anything for an honest dollar—until, in a stroke of luck late in his life, he landed a cushy government job as the night watchman at a minor federal building on the outskirts of Capitol Hill. One night, while on duty, he was murdered by intruders with his own gun. In early 1963, such an event was still rare enough that the mystery of his death and the whereabouts of the murder weapon headlined the *Star* and

Times-Herald, and even merited a small front-page column in the then normally local-news-adverse *Post.* The D.C. police, assisted by the FBI, vigorously pursued the case. Within a week, his assailants were apprehended: two boys barely in their teens—boys my age—who confessed to accidentally shooting him, after hiding in a bathroom until after closing to steal the gun from an old man they figured wouldn't put up much of a fight. No one had intended it to happen. It was a random tragedy without an author.

My grandfather's death, like all such unexpected renders in the fabric of normal life, had unforeseen consequences. When my parents fought—which they did frequently—I would sometimes come across him in the pantry, the calm in the eye of the storm, quietly advising my father on how to weather the latest squall that, like the certainty of typhoons in the tropics, he accepted as the inevitable consequence of life with someone who was, in his understated summation of my mother's character, "a little high strung." He had been the ballast of our home. Without his steadying influence, my parents' marriage floundered on the shoals of their inability to live together, and slowly and painfully went to pieces. Whenever I had money, I jumped ship for a few hours, escaping into the place that had always been there for me whenever anything went bad: the movies.

Mostly, I paid to get in with my own money, which I earned by collecting bottles for deposit refunds or by carrying groceries for overloaded shoppers coming out of the neighborhood Safeway. Occasionally, my parents paid. When my grandfather was alive, I could always ask him if all else failed; and for the price of a lecture on the virtues of self-sufficiency—which I ordinarily tried to embody—I was in. That summer, though, there was no money. It wasn't just that his funeral expenses ate up his meager death benefits and then some, but, as I figured out much later, he had helped keep our household afloat financially as well as emotionally. Having seven mouths to feed, my father took a second job, as much to be away, I suspect, as for the money. With the dog days of summer settling in, my mother, resentful of being alone, fell into a loud and angry depression, which, without the buffer of my grandfather or my father, fell upon my four younger sisters and me like a hurricane upon little houses on an exposed shore. There was nothing to do but ride out the gale as best we could. I would take refuge whenever I could in one of my storm cellars: the Lincoln, the Republic, and the Booker T., the three movie theaters on U Street, the Pennsylvania Avenue of black Washington. But, more and more frequently, I would spend my money on ice cream from the alcoholic Good Humor man, whose otherwise unpredictable appearances were somehow synchronized to the days my mother would spend her last dime on a fountain Coke for herself—which she'd make me run to the drugstore to buy—convinced that Coke syrup soothed the ulcers my sisters and I were giving her. The two littlest of my sisters would cry because they couldn't have ice cream. My mother would yell at them for crying. And I would buy them ice cream with my money because they generally kept their promises to shut up if I did.

But, as predictably as some no-account lover in one of my grandfather's Bessie Smith records, the day I most needed my money, it was gone: a day when I was awakened by my mother screaming at my father for not leaving her enough money to even buy a fountain Coke; a day the Good Humor man, of course, showed up like some mocking angel of financial death, and caused my sisters to cry without relief; a day I needed the shelter of a movie. I scoured the neighborhood for bottles to little avail. And Saturday, the big shopping day at Safeway, was a distant shore, an eternity away. As I stood in front of the Lincoln, the big-screen flagship of the three theaters, I was certain of two things: that the title on the marquee spoke to my deepest desire, and that there was only one way I was going to see the *Great Escape*—I'd have to sneak into the theater.

Waiting by the alley door, I little appreciated the irony of breaking into the movies to watch the breakout from Stalag Luft III because my heart was pounding so hard I was certain the heaving of my chest would betray me to the usher, as he let out the patrons from the previous show. But when the door opened with a sudden, ominous creak, an attractive woman was first out. The usher's eyes zeroed in on her rear end like a Tex Avery wolf's, and I knew I had suddenly become invisible. When I got inside, I snagged a ticket stub off the floor, just to be on the safe side. But I did not feel truly safe until the lights went down, and, enveloped in the cool darkness, I was transported to another world. I didn't know then that it was a world created by a screenwriter, anymore than I could know that I would grow up to be one, or that this day would be one of the reasons why. What I knew was that it was a world that made sense, where tragic deaths only came in the service of noble causes. And though I also knew that was a lie, it somehow made the truth bearable. I saw the movie twice.

———————

WGA, Emmy, and Humanitas Award nominee **Daryl G. Nickens** chairs the graduate screenwriting program at the American Film Institute.

GAIL PARENT

THE FIRST TIME ... I stood on the table in the writer's room, I stood with such confidence that the eleven male writers didn't even attempt to look up my dress.

Flashback: The very day Kenny Soms, my writing partner at the time, and I first came to Hollywood to do the *Carol Burnett Show*, I lost my voice. If you believe in psychology, you would assume it was because I was new and young and shiny and scared to talk. And there I was, surrounded by seasoned writers, who pitched freely at will. They knew how to capture the rhythm of being funny on your feet, whereas I liked to write the way I ate, secretly and alone. When the writers gathered in Arnie Rosen's office, and ideas flew past me and over my head, I knew that one day they would expect my laryngitis to clear up. But it didn't and the fear of pitching grew worse. I was sure that if I were to say anything, not only would everyone turn and stare, but the word "fraud" would be whispered every time I walked down the hall. (Many writers have and have had the fear of being discovered as an untalented fraud who can fool those around them. In my case, it closed my throat and made me cry on the way to work. I didn't buy but rented a car in case I had to leave town quickly.)

That was a long time ago and fortunately, the written words I handed in were good, and slowly, slowly I eased into being a part of the room.

Flash forward: Fellow writers laughed at what I said, and exactly a hundred thousand lines that came out of my mouth went into the script. I found that there was no bigger thrill than being the one who saved the day or coming up with that perfect last joke so that exhausted people could go home. (I did not accomplish this every time I got up to bat, but there were plenty of times that I earned the game ball.)

When I first started pitching, I did it sitting down. Gradually, I stood. Usually with a big smile on my face, in anticipation of the laughter I would get. This is, after all, a sitcom writer's performance. And then late one night, in a conference room just big enough to hold a table, chairs, and fattening things, we were down to fixing the last line. The clock on the wall said it was three, but our Rolexes and Cartiers said it was three twelve and who would you believe? Tired voices struggled to get the one joke that would send us home. There were cashew nuts and M&M's spread in front of everyone. Writers, due to lack of sleep, and too much coffee, were getting raucous. The men started calling their wives to tell them they may never be home again. They stood in the corners of the room, whispering into phones, asking about the kids they hadn't seen for years. Many of the conversations ended with them looking around the room, seeing if anyone was listening, and then saying into the phone, "Me too," which meant that the woman on the other end had said, "I love you," but that they were too self-conscious to say it back. Everyone knows what "Me too" means, but it's still interesting to see a roomful of men deteriorate so quickly.

And then the muses chose me to deliver the joke that would kill. By this time the room was noisy and out of control. Everyone had chosen their poison. Vodka was poured, cigarettes were smoked and sucked, pot and coke were out in the open. Cries of help could be heard whenever one listened. Since by now it was incredibly loud in the room, I climbed onto the table, my arms outstretched, cashews stuck to the bottom of my shoes, and said, "You can all go home now. I have it!" At the prospect of getting to go home, everyone was happy, except for one man, who loathed his wife.

Eleven pairs of bloodshot eyes were on me. The hope that filled that room could have saved a life. I laughed at what I was going to say, enjoying it already. "He taps his glass ready for a toast," I began, and then launched into my triumph. "He says, 'My darling ex-wife Linda has agreed to marry me again and bear my children.' Linda says, 'I'd rather be spit on by monkeys,' and he says, 'You can have both.'"

Silence.

I slipped on a package of Marlboros as I descended the mountain. Embarrassed, I told them all that at least I had made an attempt. Then somebody said, "Put it in, it's good enough for now." And there were mumbles of agreement. So it went in the script for less than twenty-four hours. I had wanted to wow them and let them go home. All I had done was let them go home.

My story has a happy ending. I felt right about what I had done, and I never hesitated to stand on the table again.

———

Gail Parent's credits include writer for *The Carol Burnett Show,* co-creator of *Mary Hartman, Mary Hartman,* co-writer of *The Main Event,* co-executive producer/writer of *The Golden Girls,* and writer for *Tracey Takes On.*

DANIEL PETRIE, JR.

I HAVE THE Writers Guild to thank for the first time I got paid for it—even though the Writers Guild, which represents writers collectively, is not in the business of getting jobs for individual writers.

I also have to thank ICM, the famous talent agency, which *is* in the business of getting jobs for individual writers—even though they had nothing whatever to do with me getting this (or any other) writing job.

I can't explain those contradictions without giving some background; without, to use the term of art in television series development, laying some pipe.

When I first started writing screenplays, just out of college, I couldn't make a living at it. I needed a day job. At length I landed a job in the mail room at ICM. My plan was to save half of my salary for six months, then quit ICM and go back to writing, living on the other half of the salary for another six months.

There were a couple of flaws in this plan. First, it turned out that I was unable to save half—or $57.50—of my $115-a-week starting pay. In fact, I somehow didn't manage to save any of it.

The second flaw in the plan revolved around my not understanding the entire premise of the mail room. It's not the kind of job taken by people who need a day job. Rather, it's an entry-level hell-week job entered into only by people who have the goal of getting out of the mail room and into the larger business of the firm. That premise, it turned out, was understood by everyone in the business, even understood by anyone who ever read a book about the business—except, of course, for me. But almost immediately, like a hostage bonding with his captors, I internalized the work-really-hard-and-get-out-of-the-mail-room ethic, almost forgetting the larger goal of becoming a writer.

I wound up staying at ICM for five years, going from mailroom guy to reader to assistant to agent.

Yes. I was an agent. As you can imagine, those aren't the easiest words to write. Nevertheless, I feel in this age of greater understanding and openness, I can come out, as it were, about this aspect of my past.

During this five-year stretch, I met and married my wife, who was kind and brave enough to encourage my latent ambition to be a writer. But I still hadn't saved any money. So I couldn't quit ICM; if I did, even with my wife working, I'd have had to get a real job again right away. I needed to have access to that great patron of the arts, unemployment insurance. In short, I needed to get fired.

That's the reason I owe thanks to ICM for the start of my career: Eventually, thank God, ICM finally fired me. I started writing again. Eventually I was happy enough with a script to show it to some of my ex-clients. Encouraged by my writer friends, I gave the script to a wonderful producer, Marcia Nasatir, who had been an agent and a studio executive, and who was and remains a pioneering role model for women in the industry.

The day before talking to me about my script, Marcia had talked with Robert Wunsch, whom I had known when I was an agent, and he was a vice president at United Artists, a post which Marcia herself had once held.

I knew that Bob Wunsch had been an agent before he became first a producer, then an executive; Marcia told me something I didn't know: Bob was going back into the agency business and had just started his own agency. This had happened so recently that Bob had no clients. Which is a good thing for me, since that script might not have been strong enough to get Bob to sign me if he had a full client list. Marcia sent my script to Bob, who read it, liked it, and signed me as a client.

That first script has not sold to this day, but a year later I gave Bob a much better script. Bob sold it over one weekend—this script was filmed three years later as *The Big Easy*—and, using that script as a writing sample, Bob got me my first studio writing job, a rewrite on *Beverly Hills Cop*, which was then in development hell at Paramount. I wound up getting sole screenplay credit on *Cop*, and Bob Wunsch represented me until his retirement.

But neither of those was the first time I got paid for it. After the first draft of the script that became *The Big Easy* was done, I was just about at the end of the ICM severance pay and the unemployment insurance was about to run out. I thought I'd have to get a real job before doing the rewrites that would make the script what I hoped it could be.

That's when the Writers Guild rescued me. You see, since I'd never sold anything, or been hired to write anything, I wasn't a member of the WGA. And the WGA establishes minimums of compensation below which Writers Guild members cannot work. Thus it was that when director Jeremy Kagan was developing a screenplay for a foreign producer who was not signatory to the WGA agreement, and in any case could not afford the WGA minimum pay, he needed to hire a writer who was not in the WGA. Bob Wunsch suggested me. It was major rewrite for $7,500 and the movie never got made, but I was thrilled to get the job. It kept me going long enough to finish the script that got me the first studio job that in turn got me into the Writers Guild.

I've had many reasons to thank the Writers Guild in the 18 years since then, but I'll always be particularly grateful for the Guild's backhanded role in the first time I got paid for it.

———————

Daniel Petrie, Jr. is currently the vice president of the Writers Guild of America, west, and served a term as president from 1997 through September 1999.

An Academy Award® nominee for his screenplay of *Beverly Hills Cop,* Petrie also wrote *The Big Easy,* co-wrote and produced *Shoot to Kill,* co-wrote and executive produced *Turner & Hooch,* co-wrote and directed *Toy Soldiers* and *In the Army Now,* and directed *Dead Silence* for HBO. Petrie also serves on the Board of Governors of the Academy of Motion Pictures Arts and Sciences and is chair of the Academy's Writers Branch Executive Committee.

ANNA HAMILTON PHELAN

THE FIRST TIME I saw my first agent, he was sitting behind his desk looking at me over his glasses. I was in his outer office trying to get his secretary (this was the pre-assistant '60's) to accept a one-act play I'd written. Her intercom buzzed. She leaned into it and shouted, "A playwright (chuckle) and classical actress (big chuckle). No professional credits. College stuff."

The next minute my first agent, who was in his sixties at the time, was waving me into his office in the Brill Building on Broadway in New York City. My friends were coming up zip after months and months in the get-an-agent marathon. I had scored one, a well-regarded one, yet, after walking my one-acts and my audition monologues and my 8 x 10 glossies around the city for one week. (Gloat. Gloat.) Talent will out, I thought. The fact that he hadn't read a word I'd written or ever seen me act didn't figure in my logic.

"You're gonna have to bug me," my first agent said. "You're gonna have to pester me and push me and be a real pain in the ass or I'm gonna forget you real fast. You got that?"

"Un-huh. I think so."

"Good, because that's your job. You do your job and I'll do mine."

I did and he did. He got me my first scribe-for-money gigs writing audition material for actors. Since I'd been writing my own audition monologues, it was a natural. For fifteen dollars you got a three-minute dramatic monologue tailored to your very own personality, honed to showcase your particular attributes as a performer. It was twenty-five dollars for a comedy piece because they took me longer. A two-character scene went for thirty-five bucks. Years later when the Universal toppers insisted Cher audition for *Mask,* I wrote her a five-minute screen test as the character in the movie so she could play every emotional beat the character played in the entire screenplay. It was like watching a multiple personality on a binge, but she blew them away and got the part.

My first agent secured acting work for me in summer stock and dinner theater. *Antigone,* it wasn't. Poppy Matson in *The Tender Trap* and Katrin Sveg in *The Marriage Go-Round,* it was. But these acting gigs led to commercial work, which paid the rent so I could write. And he never stopped encouraging me to write, write, write. He said something good might click in, even though most of it would probably be awful. And mostly it was awful.

He sat on crates and folding chairs in musty, dusty Off-Off-Broadway theaters (spaces) and suffered through my first produced plays. When the work improved, he nudged producers to read it, to go and see it performed.

He truly took me under his wing, his family's wing. I had Sunday dinners with them, attended the theater with them, sat at their Passover seder tables. I became close to his wife, a lovely, gracious woman. I became friends with his children and grandchildren. All the while he continued to work hard for me as an agent. He encouraged me to go to Hollywood and write for the movies. I did. He told me I should someday write a book for a Broadway musical. I am.

Years after he had retired from agenting and was in ill health, I had dinner with him in New York. I asked him whatever possessed him to represent me, a 21-year-old with no credits or experience who walked in off the street in white go-go boots.

"You looked like Kathleen Monahan."

"Who's Kathleen Monahan?"

"The first girl I ever shtupped."

"What!? What did that have to do with me!?"

"Nothing."

My first agent taught me an important lesson. Very often in this crazy business what we think has to do with us, both the negative and positive, doesn't at all.

Anna Hamilton Phelan's feature film credits include *Mask* (nominated by the WGA as Best Original Screenplay) and *Gorillas in the Mist* (Academy Award® nomination for Best Screenplay Adaptation).

ALAN PLATER

THE FIRST TELEVISION PLAY

THE FIRST TIME I had a television credit was in the early 1960s, for a play called *The Referees*. At the time I was making a sort of living as an uninspired and discontented architect in the north of England. I had written five earlier television plays that nobody wanted. If you stripped away the jokes and the fancy writing they were mostly about discontented architects with a recurring central character who was generally a crumpled young man with the soul of a poet.

The Referees was different, mainly because of Mike, a kid I'd been to school with. When he was sixteen he did a very good Mario Lanza impersonation but calculated this didn't represent too much in the way of career prospects so he went to university and got a degree in modern languages.

Mike was determined not to spend his life teaching modern languages and took a job selling scales to shopkeepers. In those days grocers used scales for weighing out butter, sugar and other domestic items.

One day Mike called round and dragged me willingly from my drawing board.

"I'm getting out of scales," he said. "Everything's prepackaged and grocers don't have to weigh anything anymore."

"Yes," I said, "I think I've noticed that."

"So I'm changing jobs. Will you write me a reference?"

"Me? Why me?"

"You're a qualified architect and you've had a play on the radio. That makes you respectable."

"Nobody's ever called me respectable before, least of all you, Mike. And nobody's ever asked me to write a reference. What do you want me to say?"

"That I'm sober, clean-living, honest and trustworthy."

"Easy," I said. "Not entirely true but easy. What's the job you're applying for?"

"I'm going to sell baconslicers."

It seemed obvious to me that he'd misread the market and selling baconslicers was even crazier than selling scales but that wasn't my business. Mike had done me the honor of thinking I was respectable so I wrote the reference, he got the job and the next time I saw him, thirty-five years later, he was teaching modern languages.

After Mike left, the idea for the play took hold. A crumpled young man with the soul of a poet goes for a job interview. He gets the job but as he's leaving the boss says: "You'll let me have your references in the morning?"

The young man, trying to cover his confusion, says: "Er . . . yes. How many?"

"Three's normal, isn't it?"

And that was the plot. A young man in a strange town has twenty-four hours to find three people who will testify to his goodness. We never find out why he's in a strange town or what the job is or what the firm makes or does. Nobody bothered with back stories in those days; as a matter of fact, I still don't. Audiences don't care, either.

Naturally, nobody in the strange town will write references for the young man. His poetic soul puts them off. Our boy gets drunk, depressed and wakes up in a filthy doss-house where a harmless lunatic (my plays have always been densely populated with harmless lunatics) forges the three references. Next morning, our young man delivers the references, gets the job and makes a date with the girl in the front office.

I sent the play to a lovely man called Vivian Daniels, who at that time produced television plays for the BBC Network, working out of an old church hall in Manchester. Vivian did the lot: producer and director and script editor. Script editors hadn't yet been invented on our side of the Atlantic, though they were heading our way on the Gulf Stream. Vivian had read and turned down some of the earlier plays, mainly because of their unrelenting jokes. "After a while," he used to say, "your jauntiness becomes resistible."

But this time, seemingly, I'd controlled the jauntiness and the BBC bought *The Referees* for a fee of £150.

There were a few twitchy moments along the way.

The first was when Vivian said to me: "I'd like to cast an actor called Donald Churchill in the lead, if you don't mind."

"Why should I mind?"

"He stammers."

To be sure, Don had a slight hesitation in his speech which he used, very adroitly, to echo the uncertainty within the character. He later acted in other of my plays and became a successful writer himself. He died much too young, though he subsequently set a record that would have pleased him by having a stage play rejected by a London fringe theater seven years after his death.

The next twitchy moment was during a break in the studio rehearsals when Harold Lang, a fine eccentric character actor who was playing the harmless lunatic, said to me: "I'd like to talk to you about my character."

"I think he's a harmless lunatic," I said.

"But there has to be more . . ."

Fortunately, Harold was called back to rehearsal before he could finish the sentence and he never did. It was a great relief. Nobody had told me that actors wanting to talk about their characters was part of the job and to this day I've never been sure what to tell them. Writing is one thing; behaving like a writer is something else and there are no reliable books on how to do it. This might be the one.

In the early 1960s there were two or three plays on BBC television every week and as many again on the commercial channel. Nobody got rich writing them but we all had fun making them. They were all studio-based. It was an innocent era when you had total freedom to tell any story you liked, as long as it could fit into, say, eight studio sets and a couple of corners.

The sets were made out of wood, canvas, paint, ticky-tacky and blind faith. I walked around the studio set of *The Referees* and was dismayed to find written on the back of a brick wall the words "Harry Worth Show"—a very popular sitcom of the period. I thought the BBC might have pushed the boat out and made me a brick wall of my very own, but naturally I didn't say anything. This is the first time I've talked about it openly.

Telerecording had just arrived on the scene but editing was an expensive luxury. The normal process was to record the play in two or three chunks. If anything went wrong, the actors went back to the beginning of the relevant chunk and did it all over again. The tape was then glued together (literally, I believe) to make an hour-long piece.

It was still a cottage industry. A year or so after writing *The Referees* I started contributing to *Z Cars*, the pioneering cop show, a series that continued to go out live until 1966. The theory was that actors performed with greater urgency and immediacy if they were scared shitless. Old actors still argue about this.

There was a ten-day gap between the recording of *The Referees* and its transmission. At this point, global considerations took over. Why? Because all this happened at the height of the Cuban missile crisis.

After we'd recorded the play I walked back to the funny little hotel I was staying in along the road—it was full of traveling salesmen, northern English variations on Willy Loman, who sat around the lounge each evening in a numbed silence. The place was run by a woman who claimed to be Elia Kazan's cousin (is it any wonder my plays come out wacky?) and as I walked along Dickenson Road my thoughts hovered in a black hole roughly equidistant from Kennedy, Krushchev and my play.

I murmured something along the lines of:

"Now listen, whoever's listening. I am a devout atheist so this is not to be regarded as a prayer under any circumstances. But if there are any cosmic forces out there with influence in high places, please ask them not to drop any nuclear weapons until

after the play's gone out. I don't want to be incinerated. I'm aller-
gic to incineration. But if you must drop the things, have the de-
cency to wait ten days, okay? At least let me be incinerated with
one television credit."

Vanity of vanities, all is vanity.

But as we know, it worked. It illustrates the simple truth that,
as writers, what we do is the most important thing in the world
and, simultaneously, it doesn't matter a damn. What could be
simpler? There's another odd contradiction. The Cuban missile
crisis took place in October 1962. But according to my credits list,
The Referees was shown in 1961.

This is not something anyone should worry about. This is the
tale as I remember it and, as Mr. John Ford almost said, if in
doubt write the legend. This is the legend of my first time.

Alan Plater has been a full-time writer since 1961, with over 200 assorted credits in radio, televi-
sion, theater, and films—plus six novels, occasional journalism, broadcasting, and teaching. His
work includes *The Barchester Chronicles, The Beiderbecke Trilogy, Fortunes of War,* and *A Very
British Coup*—accumulating awards from, among others, the Broadcasting Press Guild and the
Royal Television Society—plus an International Emmy (USA), the Golden Fleece of Georgia
(USSR), and the Grand Prix of the Banff Festival. He was president of the Writers Guild of Great
Britain from September 1991 until April 1995.

CARL REINER

INCENTIVE

IN THE SPRING of 1958 I received a check for a thousand dollars which, at that point in my life, was the most satisfying thousand dollars I had ever earned. I had been paid a fairly decent wage for my efforts as an actor on the Broadway stage and for appearances on television but it was *the first time* anyone had ever offered me money to write something. At the time I was happily employed as an actor on *Sid Caesar Invites You,* one of the later incarnations of the celebrated *Your Show of Shows* (1950–1954), and had spent seven years in the now legendary writer's room, contributing to the creative effort as best I could. I thought of myself and was accepted as a writer without portfolio. Whenever I would come up with a less-than-brilliant joke, it would gently be batted down by one of the more tactful writers who enjoyed reminding me that I "was nothing but a f—n' actor!" Very soon after, thanks to that admonition, I found myself sitting alone in the basement den of my New Rochelle home, writing short stories. Thirteen years earlier, during the war, I had been assigned to the U.S. Signal Corps where I was trained to be a teletype operator. Wondering if I could still type, I dusted off my wife's old, manual Smith-Corona, rolled in a sheet of paper and tested myself by quickly typing the traditional:

"Noq is thc time fr a;; goood mem to comr to the aaid of thier patty." I was happy to discover that I had lost none of my typing skills. After practicing for a few minutes, I was able to negotiate a pretty neat, "Now is the tine for all good mem to comw to the aid of thire psryt." By the end of the evening, I had written a dozen perfect "Now is the time for all good men to come to the aid of their party" plus a rather humorous and touching, four-page story about an old woman who, to prove she was not getting senile, and could fend for herself, struggled to shop for and cook an elaborate, four-course Friday dinner for her son and daughter-in-law, only to discover that she had cooked the meal a week too soon. The next night I wrote a five-page story about a Little League game where a boorish, loudmouthed father shouted instructions to his son, the pitcher, on how to intimidate the scrawny, ten-year-old batter he was facing.

"Throw at his head . . . stuff it in his ear," he hollered, "or I don't buy you no hamburger after the game!"

In a couple of weeks I had amassed about a dozen or so pieces. My wife, who, I trusted would tell me the truth, read them and convinced me that they were really good. Armed with her positive response, I gave them to my literate, college-educated friend and neighbor, the successful textile manufacturer, Julian Rochelle. He called the following day and couldn't have been more supportive. He said that he liked the stories very much and asked if I minded if he passed them along to this buddy of his who made pocket-books. He was sure the guy would get a kick out of them. Pleased that Julian thought my literary efforts were worthy of being read by strangers, I, of course, gave him my permission to pass them on. A week or so later, at a party at Julian's house, this man sought me out and told me how much he enjoyed my stories and asked if I would join him for lunch that week. I mumbled something about checking my calendar and scooted away to join my host Julian at the buffet table. I asked Julian if he would be upset if I declined his friend's offer to lunch. Julian said that it might be good for me to have lunch with the guy.

"He really enjoyed your stories," Julian reiterated.

"Do authors eat lunch with everybody who likes their writing?" I asked.

"No, but this guy might be able to do something for you," he suggested.

"What'll he do for me," I asked, "give me a wholesale price on a lizard pocketbook?"

I had assumed that the man was a customer who bought Julian's textiles to use for pocketbook linings. Julian laughed and quietly explained that his friend was an executive at Simon and Schuster's Pocket Books division.

At lunch that Monday, the gentleman, whose name I wish I could remember, asked me what I had planned to do with my stories. In those days, the softcover Pocket Books sold for thirty-five cents and I told him I hoped to write thirty-five short stories and have a book titled "A Penny a Story." He informed me that he was not looking for books of short stories, but if I was serious about being published, he would be interested in my writing a novel. I explained that I had no idea of how to write a novel and he casually suggested that I simply take one of my stories and enlarge it. I pointed out to him that the longest of my stories was nine pages and he suggested that I just add a hundred and fifty more. He said that if I agreed to do that, he would offer me a contract and a thousand-dollar advance and added that I could take as much time as I want. I quickly accepted the offer but insisted that he give me a tight deadline. I explained that like a lot of people in live television, I work best under pressure. We decided that I would have eight weeks to plump up one of my short stories. I chose a story called "Twenty-three Arthur Barringtons," and six weeks later, I delivered it to the editor, who suggested we change the title to *Enter Laughing*. It was published later that year and to his everlasting credit, the *Show of Shows'* writer who had reminded me that I was "nothing but a f—n' actor" (to protect the other writers in the writer's room, we will simply refer to this writer as Mel Tolkin) happily informed me that I was also "f—n' *good* writer!"

Along with the first kiss and the first sexual encounter, getting a thousand-dollar advance to write a novel was right up there with the other big thrills of my life.

Depending on who you talk to, **Carl Reiner** is best known as a co-star on the renowned television program *Your Show of Shows* . . . or as the creator, writer, director, and co-star of *The Dick Van Dyke Show* . . . or as The Interviewer of *The 2000 Year Old Man* . . . or as director of feature films, including *The Jerk, All of Me,* and *Oh, God!* . . . or as the winner of twelve Emmys . . . or as the writer of books including *Enter Laughing, All Kinds of Love,* and *How Paul Robeson Saved My Life, and Other Mostly Happy Stories;* and screenplays for *The Thrill of It All, Dead Men Don't Wear Plaid,* and *Bert Rigby, You're a Fool* . . . or simply as a show business legend who, after more than fifty years of making us laugh, is still writing, directing, and performing.

DEL REISMAN

THE FIRST TIME I KNEW MOVIES WERE WRITTEN

OUR FAMILY CAR was a used Ford with a rumble seat, bought by our mother from a dealer who told her it had been driven by a "little old lady from Pasadena." It may have been the first time that glorious phrase was used to sell a car.

My kid sister and I knew our car; we understood it. Its engine had an unmistakable sound. We recognized it like we recognized the barks of dogs in our neighborhood. So we knew when our mother was coming home from work.

One evening, that raucous sound came down Sweetzer Avenue in what is now called "West" Hollywood (cheaper rents than Hollywood). We lived in an apartment which was a unit in one of those courts Nathanael West wrote about.

We rushed outside through the high weeds of the vacant lot next to us. Our mother pulled up and shouted, "Get Mr. Athey," a neighbor who made himself available to help with heavy lifting. We got Mr. Athey, a lean, muscular man, and the two of us, at her direction, carefully lifted a studio-owned Underwood typewriter, the big standard model, out of the rumble seat and lugged it inside.

After dinner, she sat down to work and typed page after page of . . . what did she call it? Script. She typed pages that had been handed to her by someone at the studio. A writer's pages, not all of them legible, except to the practiced eye of a secretary.

I knew what she was typing. I looked over her shoulder. On the pages people talked to each other, saying the kinds of things that I had heard coming from the screen before. Funny words, threatening words, words I didn't understand. They were all playacting words to me, and I loved their familiarity.

I understood, of course, that all those words added up to a movie. Once in a while, my mother would make a typing mistake. I waited impatiently while she pulled back six carbons and carefully erased the offending word, or perhaps the offending letter. Then, with what seemed to me to be surgical skill, she fixed the error and got on with it. That slowdown gave me the chance to read the words again.

I liked the smart-ass talk. Men and women snapping at each other. How did they think of those things?

When I finally got to sleep, I dreamed up my own movie, based on the pages I had read.

It was the time of the depression. Real movies took us out of the constant worry about money, or rather the lack of it. They showed us penthouses and nightclubs and white telephones (in fact, the studios called certain movies White Telephone Movies).

In the morning, Mr. Athey and I lugged the typewriter out to the rumble seat. Once at work, at the old Universal (Carl Laemmle's Universal, then Charles Rogers's Universal, then Nate

Blumberg's Universal), my mother got one of the guards at the gate to lug it back to her office.

A couple days later I walked over to the Fox Carmel at Santa Monica and Crescent Heights to see the Saturday matinee, the highlight of my week. Four hours of cartoons, a newsreel, maybe a March of Time, a Republic Western, some kind of a kid contest onstage, and finally, a feature.

At the candy stand, I collected all my neighborhood pals and as we chomped on Abba-Zabba bars, I told them that the people on the screen didn't make up what they said to each other, that people called screenwriters wrote down the words first.

They didn't want to hear it.

But something magical happened. Once the movies started, I lost myself in the illusions, forgetting completely about my mother's typing; the word "script" never entered my mind.

That disassociation became my way to involve myself in the stories.

Years later, many years later, I still do it. Knowing what I know, knowing what I've done with my own Underwoods and my own pencils, I sit in a theater and let the process take over.

I like the movies.

––––––––

Del Reisman (past-president, Writers Guild of America, west, 1991–1993) began his professional writing career in live television in the 1950s. He was story editor for the original live show *Playhouse 90* for producer Martin Manulis and the original *Twilight Zone* for producer/creator Rod Serling. Later he was story editor/writer/producer for the television series *The Untouchables, Rawhide,* and *Man in the City,* among others. Mr. Reisman is a current member of the screenwriting faculty of the American Film Institute and a member of the National Film Preservation Board, Library of Congress.

GARY ROSS

I SUPPOSE, looking back on it, the "first time" for anything is filled with lots of nostalgia and none of the trauma that actually accompanies the event. My first professional writing experience is no exception—although I do still get a weird knot in my stomach every time I look at the dollar/franc conversion rate. I'd better explain:

My father was also a screenwriter *(Creature from the Black Lagoon, Brubaker, The Great Race)*. Naturally, I tried to avoid working in Hollywood for as long as I possibly could. I wanted to forge my own identity and work in a different medium and, for me, that meant becoming a novelist. Actually, it meant smoking lots of Gauloise cigarettes and hanging out in coffeehouses till two in the morning, but I was in that vulnerable part of a career where cliché tends to supplant experience. Of course, none of this lasted, and, when the moment finally came to sit down and begin a book, I took the same deep breath that anyone takes who must first call themselves a writer, and then ultimately become one.

I began to type.

Honestly, it was torture for me. I was a very outgoing person (especially at that age) and my sociable nature combined with the hormones of my early twenties made it difficult to sit still for very long. Nonetheless I finally completed a first novel and when that didn't sell, I began another one.

The isolation was murder. When all my friends were getting up in the morning and going to their first jobs, I was getting up, and going over to my desk. I was living in a complete vacuum—first on faith and then eventually on fumes. I had friends who were working on television shows: making a lot of money and getting a great deal of validation. I was making no money and getting my phone shut off. To compensate for this inequity, I would read my daily output (three or four pages) to a not-so-small circle of friends who were kind enough to give me the encouragement to continue.

I finally completed a hundred pages of the novel and a detailed outline for the remainder. I phoned an old college roommate who had since joined his father's literary agency, and he assured me it would be enough to get a publishing deal—if, indeed, there was a publishing deal to be had. So we sent out the manuscript and I spent the next several weeks marking the passage of time in minutes. Every time the phone rang my pulse jumped: like some imaginary bailiff had stuck his head into my life to announce that the "jury was in."

Of course, it was more than just the desire to sell something. I was in that horrible blind spot where every writer lives at the beginning of a career. Sure, *I* had faith in my writing ability but maybe it was just delusional. Maybe the compliments of friends were just acts of kindness, or worse: a well-intentioned web of lies, designed only to keep me from suicide. The problem is you just don't know. There is so much bravado required to overcome this early uncertainty that perspective is virtually nonexistent. I would experience wild pendulum swings. I was a genius. I was a fool. I was a craftsman. I was a hack. I was better than what I just read. I could never live up to what I just read. I envied. I scoffed. I dreamed. I despaired. I felt vitally alive. I felt hopelessly dead. I finally got a phone call.

Tom Congdon had been the editor in chief of Doubleday for years and had just started his own publishing house. It was called Congdon/Lates and was funded through some French investors based in Paris. He loved the novel. He was excited about me as an author. He was offering me a publishing contract. *This was the man who found* Jaws! I was elated. I was proud. Naturally, I was terrified. The next couple of weeks were spent wondering if each sentence was a "professional" sentence worthy of being edited by the man who had discovered *Jaws.* In really obsessive moments I wondered if each word was "professional," or if there was a more "professional" choice that hadn't occurred to me since, of course, I was not yet a "professional." The only problem is that while I was wondering all of this, Tom Congdon was going bankrupt.

When François Mitterrand got elected in France he was the first socialist to take power in Western Europe since the end of World War II. In addition to implementing some strict monetary policies he had terrified the international financial community merely with his existence. Was France becoming socialist? Would the rest of Europe follow? Within several months the franc had lost 50 percent of its value relative to the dollar. Good time to travel. Bad time to publish. Tom Congdon's funding was all in French francs and he suddenly had half as much money to buy books. For a while I just assumed he was busy when he didn't return my phone calls. When he didn't return my agent's phone calls, I was getting concerned, but I chalked it up to youthful insecurity. When he finally refused to pay me my start money, I knew that something was wrong.

After a little while we received the letter. It was polite, sincere, contrite and unambiguous. My two-month honeymoon as a "professional" writer was over. At least it was going to have a profound hiatus. I tried to remain philosophical about all of this (*The Myth of Sisyphus* helped in particular) but after a while my spirits began to flag. We tried to sell the book again on the open market, but, much like Hollywood, no one likes their "hot properties" slightly used. I still refused to give up. I kept working on the manuscript, figuring I would sell it as a finished work when the book was finally completed, but I started to go broke. A four-day appearance on a game show (*Tic-Tac-Dough*) helped for a while, but the money didn't last. Before long, taxes and generosity had claimed most of my winnings. (I hung out with a lot of actors back then and they weren't exactly forthcoming about picking up a dinner check.) I was on page three hundred without a publisher in sight and my windfall had turned into a stipend.

That's when a friend of mine asked me if I wanted to write a treatment with him for Paramount. He was a phenomenally talented hustler and had gotten them to buy an idea about a local TV anchor who discovers an impending global nuclear confrontation. What the hell. They were going to pay me the same amount for thirty pages as Tom Congdon would have for seven hundred. Suddenly, the movie business didn't feel quite as evil.

Autonomy from my father seemed less important than autonomy from my creditors. I wrote the treatment in a few weeks and
put both our names on it (a piece of personal exploitation I
didn't fully understand until later). Through all of this, of course,
I intended to go back and finish the book—in fact, I still had the
filing cards of the outline plastered across my bulletin board. But
not long after that, another friend read the treatment and offered
me a job writing a screenplay. This one paid way more than the
novel and by my third job, I succumbed to the inevitable and
took down the file cards.

Was all of this a blessing? Was it a curse? It's hard to know.
I've had a very fulfilling career in the movies but it was never my
childhood dream. Literary lions were the men that I idolized:
Joyce, Hemingway, Faulkner, Dostoyevsky. . . . Movie stars and
filmmakers were what I grew up with. This was a blessing because I never revered them. It was a curse because I never got to.
In a sense I went into the family business. I live in the neighborhood where I grew up and my children play in the same park
where I ran around as a child. A poster for my father's movie
Creature from the Black Lagoon still hangs in the Universal com-
missary and on more than one occasion I have noticed my son
"directing" the other children in a sandbox. Maybe all of this was
inevitable, just a product of where I came from.

Not really like a family butcher shop—probably more like the
Flying Wallendas.

————

Gary Ross is screenwriter/director/producer of the Academy Award®—nominated film
Pleasantville, and the screenwriter of the films *Big* and *Dave,* both nominated for Academy

Awards® as well. *Dave* won the Paul Selvin Award from the Writers Guild of America, given to the screenplay that most embodies the spirit of civil liberties and free speech. Ross served as the president of the Los Angeles Library Commission from 1993 to 1997, overseeing its transition from a pretechnological to an information-based library system. He has also written speeches and produced television commercials for a variety of political candidates and written various political essays and op-ed pieces.

JAN SARDI

COMING TO AMERICA

THE FIRST TIME I came to America I was warned. "Expect the worst," they said. They were right. When I arrived in Park City, Utah, it was in the middle of a blizzard which had dumped ten feet of snow in the last couple of days. Having come directly from an Australian summer I couldn't imagine anywhere colder on earth. Or a stranger place to have a film festival.

It had been six weeks since I got the late-night phone call to say that *Shine* had been accepted at Sundance. A work print of the unfinished film on VHS convinced festival director Geoffrey Gilmore it was good enough. This meant a mad scramble to get the film finished in time. It also meant the Sundance screening would be the very first time *Shine* would be seen by an audience anywhere in the world. I had no idea what to expect.

The first time I saw a film of mine screened in front of an audience was in 1982. It was my first feature script, drawn from my

Italian background and my experiences as a teacher in inner-city Melbourne. It was easy to write because I had nothing to prove. I'd teach during the day and come home at night and write about what happened, just lose myself for hours. I loved it. The film was called *Moving Out* and it was a modest hit in Australia.

My second time was harder. I'd had my first success, been nominated for numerous awards, which suggested to some that I knew what I was doing. But what was once effortless turned to agony as I discovered the true meaning of "THE BLANK PAGE." Somehow I muddled my way through and managed to get to THE END. The film was made, I got nominated for more awards and couldn't believe I'd managed to fool everyone once again. I was sure I'd get found out the next time. (I realize now most writers suffer from this every second day—over to you Dennis Palumbo.)

My third script was produced, so was my fourth, my fifth and my sixth. Six scripts, six movies. I'd quit teaching in 1984 after my second outing, but in the low-budget, fee-deferral world of the Australian Film Industry the only way to survive was to write television. Twelve years, six movies and around sixty hours of produced television later I was even beginning to fool myself I knew what I was doing. If there was one thing I'd learnt it was the importance of STRUCTURE. Movie number six was *Shine*.

In 1990, Scott Hicks had approached me with a project he'd been developing for several years. It was a biopic about an unknown pianist by the name of David Helfgott. Scott had written a script about David's life called *Flight of the Bumblebee* and had been unable to attract much interest in it. It was heavy on biographical detail and research and he wanted a fresh take, a new way to tell this challenging true story. I pitched him my idea of how I'd go about it and he unselfishly entrusted the writing of the screenplay to me.

The first time I proposed the title *Shine*—long before a frame was shot—everyone wanted to know what it meant. Why *Shine*? "It'll make sense once everyone sees the movie," I told them.

As confident as I was about the title, Australian filmmakers don't always count on "everyone" seeing their small, partly government-funded movies. A theatrical release at home, some sales to foreign territories and the crowning achievement of an AFI award (an Aussie Oscar) is *realistically* what we hope for in a movie universe dominated by planet Hollywood. And just like everyone else in the movie business, we dream . . .

Fast-forward to Sundance, 1996. Producer Jane Scott had managed the impossible of getting a print ready in time, just as she'd managed to pull together the deals to make the film happen a couple of years earlier. We'd heard there were lots of parties at Sundance and night skiing and we wondered what would happen if no one turned up at the WORLD PREMIERE of our barely finished film. Scott, Jane and I had arrived the day before and had ventured to a chalet for a big party. We knew no one and no one knew us and so after an hour or so of wandering around and feeling invisible we left and had an early night.

Our initial fears that no one would turn up to the first screening were allayed when we arrived at the Egyptian on Sunday night. There was a queue waiting for standby tickets and a crowd in the foyer. It's hard to describe the feeling as the lights dimmed. We knew we'd made the film we wanted to make but had no idea of how it would go over with an audience, let alone twelve thousand miles from home. A hundred minutes later we knew.

Even as we stood on the stage to an ovation which went on

for many minutes, I don't think any of us knew what it really meant. We stepped off the stage and were surrounded. Someone reached out and tapped me on the shoulder.

"This movie is the sleeper of the festival," the man said and then hurried away.

"Do you know who that was?" asked another man with glasses and curly hair. I had no idea. "That was Kenneth Turan."

"Really, who's he?" I was a long way from home, remember?

So the man told me and introduced himself as Paul. Paul spoke very fast and gave me his card. He was an agent. "People are going to be parachuting around you I hope you realize." I didn't catch on. None of us did. Our lives had changed and we didn't know it. We went to dinner, relieved *Shine* had gone down well at its first-ever screening. There would be another the following morning, after which I planned to relax and see as many movies as possible before flying back to Australia at the end of the week.

I was feeling more at ease before the second Sundance screening. The venue was bigger and there were more people crowded in. Overnight, expectations had built and word had got around. But about twenty minutes in people started to get up and leave and then come back minutes later. It was constant. I couldn't believe it. I know it was cold outside but do Americans have such weak bladders, I wondered. A woman stood up in front of me. She continued to watch the movie as she slowly edged her way to the aisle. "Hurry it up," I wanted to tell her, "there's a good bit coming up." Sure enough, she left and came back a few minutes later—having missed the scene of David's triumph in London. "Serves you right," I thought to myself.

What I didn't know was that she was the president of Fine

Line Pictures and we'd be having lunch with her the next day. I soon discovered what all the goings and comings were about. Deals. The race to acquire the film for American distribution had begun, even before it had finished screening. These people weren't hurrying to use the bathroom; they were hurrying to use the phone.

With seven studios bidding for the American rights, the frenzy that erupted in the wake of *Shine*'s two screenings made the front pages of *Variety* and the *Hollywood Reporter* thanks to the shoot-out between Fine Line and Miramax. Thinking he'd got the rights to *Shine*, Miramax supremo Harvey Weinstein got angry instead when he discovered he'd lost out to Fine Line. He subsequently caused a scene in a local restaurant and was asked to leave. Two days later he got to share European rights to *Shine* with Buena Vista and called a press conference to announce it—in the very same restaurant he was evicted from less than forty-eight hours earlier. We met there and shook hands and he enthusiastically had one of his people take my number.

It had been three days since we'd arrived at Sundance in complete anonymity, now everyone wanted to know us. People stopped us wherever we went. One guy pitched me an idea for a movie about a disturbed pianist and wanted to know if I'd be interested in writing it. (Huh?) A couple introduced themselves as producers and said the sequel to *Shine*—"The David and Gillian Story"—would make an even better movie and they were interested in producing it. We all had at least one experience of a well-wisher stopping us in the street and bursting into tears.

And then of course there were the agents, the managers, the attorneys and the talent scouts. One agent insisted on buying me a meal. I ate it while he talked, never stopped talking, even to breath it seemed. After thirty minutes he picked up a butter knife and said he'd cut off his right arm there and then if I'd sign with him. He sounded like he meant it. By the fifth day, Jane and I couldn't take anymore. Scott had already left. He was in the middle of making a documentary and had to get back to it in a hurry. Harvey let him take the Miramax jet, believe it or not.

And so here I am, four years, one hit, seven Oscar nominations and three studio assignments later—and not one of them has been made. Everyone tells me what great scripts they are—two have got directors attached—and still the offers keep coming. I'm not complaining, not at all. Recently, I reminded my U.S. agent how I'd had six movies produced in twelve years in Australia and not one in America. "Welcome to Hollywood," came the reply. Right now I'm writing an Australian movie. I know it'll get made.

Harvey still hasn't called, though we did bump into each other at the Oscars and the BAFTA tea party and once in New York. I like him, he's a passionate man who loves his movies and is prepared to take a risk. It's a pity there's not more like him in Hollywood.

———

Jan Sardi has had six feature films produced including *Ground Zero* and the multiaward-winning *Shine*. His screenplay for *Shine* was nominated for an Academy Award®, a WGA award, and a BAFTA. Jan also won the Best Screenplay award for *Shine* at the Australian Writers Guild Awards and Australian Film Institute Awards. In addition, Jan has won many other awards and nominations for his work in Australian television.

Jan has served in various capacities on the Australian Writers Guild and is currently a member of the AWG National Executive.

TOM SCHULMAN

THE FIRST TIME I sold a screenplay I was on my way into my then agent's office to fire him. I had to go to his office because I couldn't get him on the phone. When I arrived, his secretary told me he was out. As I marched to the elevator, cursing under my breath, my agent sauntered by.

"Hey," he said. "Did I tell you there's interest in your latest screenplay?"

"No," I replied, eyes like slits. Why I didn't say, "How could you have told me, jerk bag, you haven't returned my call in two months!" I'll never know.

"A studio's interested," he said. "Come back after lunch and we'll see what develops." Before I could ask him a thousand questions, he walked away.

After two hours of nauseous pacing outside the building, I finally went back to his office. My then agent was on the phone. He covered the receiver and said, "They've offered for two fifty. I'm asking five. We'll see what happens."

"If they don't go for five, I'll take the two fifty," I said quickly.

"You can't," he said, yawning. "We passed on two fifty. Let's see what they come back with."

"We *passed?!*" I whispered. What happened inside of me at that moment is hard to describe. After six years of writing screenplays in a vacuum, I had a mortgage, a mound of debt, and a first child on the way. Without asking me, my agent had just turned down $250,000, a huge sum in 1987, hardly chump change today.

"Will they come back?" I asked, barely audible, sinking to his couch.

"I hope so," he said.

My then agent turned his attention back to his phone. He was talking to his interior decorator. The $50,000 living room set he had ordered wasn't quite right. He didn't like the fabric. His secretary stuck in her head. The studio was calling on the other line—about my script.

"Tell them to wait," he told her. "I want another fabric for the pillows," he said into the phone. "Uh huh. What about beige chenille?"

I looked at the couch I was sitting on. Chenille. Beige. The secretary opened the door again. "They're still holding," she said.

He nodded vaguely and continued about the chenille. "How much would chenille on both couches be? What?!"

At this point, I was ready to leap out of my skin. My entire career was in the balance and he was haggling about the price of sofa covering.

"How could it be that much? The silk wasn't that much! Are you telling me chenille costs more than silk?"

"Don't you think you should take the studio's call," I pleaded.

"What do you prefer?" he asked, staring at me. "Chenille or silk? For a living room sofa?"

"Silk," I said. "Stick with the silk. Please."

"What other kind of silk do you have?" he asked his decorator. The door opened. Just as the secretary stuck in her face, he shouted at her: "I'll call them back, damn it. This is important!"

In my pocket were my car keys. I never parked in the agency lot because my Karman Ghia was so beat up that I was too embarrassed to give it to the valet. On my key ring was my Swiss Army knife. Staring daggers at him, I fingered the blade. I silently vowed that if he didn't take the studio's call by the count of ten, I would put the knife to his throat. I should have known it wouldn't be necessary. Any agent worth half his commission knows when his client's getting squirrelly.

Into the phone he said, "Could you hang on a second?" And then: "Bernie, how you doing?"

I let go of my knife and stood up. Bernie was the head of the studio.

"Sorry. Three's not enough. Listen, Bernie, I'm negotiating with somebody else on the other line. If that's your best offer, so be it . . . Of course you can get back to me."

A large drop of saliva fell out of my open mouth and landed on my shoe. I was sweating so profusely, you could smell me in San Diego.

"You just turned down $300,000!" I shouted.

Phone to his ear, he stared at me. "So how much is the Dutch silk," he said. "For both couches?"

I realized he was back on with the decorator. I sank into the chenille pillow. I was about to cry but as the saying goes, I was too old. For another forty-five minutes I sat listening to him haggle about his fabric. He priced Chinese silk, Burmese silk, Danish Muslin, and Argentine suede. By the time they settled on the beige chenille at $12 a yard, the studio had called back twice. Both times my agent had waved off their call. Finally, he called them back.

"Three fifty," they told him. "That's our final offer." He told them he'd check with his client and call them back. When he hung up the phone, I nodded yes so fast, I pulled a muscle in my neck.

"I'll call them back in a few hours," he said. "Make them sweat a little. Come on, I'll walk you out."

At the elevator, he shook my hand. "Congratulations," he smiled. "You're on the map." There was a long pause. "You came here this morning to fire me, didn't you?"

I nodded. A big grin filled his face. "Good thing you didn't," he said. "You just paid for my new pillows." The elevator door opened. I got in.

"So we're off to the races," he said. "You'll hear a lot more from me from now on. Say hello to Julie." Even though my wife's name isn't Julie, I smiled and said I would. The elevator doors closed but the truth was, I didn't need an elevator. I was so pumped up I could have floated the seven floors to the ground.

True to his word, from that day on my then agent became more attentive. The next morning his secretary called to say he didn't have time to call, but wanted me to know that the deal had closed at three fifty. I told her to thank him for the call.

A week later, he called in person. "I read most of your script last night," he said. "I liked it. I can see why they bought it."

"Thanks," I said.

To this day I hate beige chenille.

Tom Schulman wrote *Dead Poets Society* for which he received a Writers Guild Award nomination and an Academy Award®. He also wrote *Honey, I Shrunk the Kids, What About Bob?, Medicine Man, Eight Heads in a Duffel Bag,* and *Holy Man.*

MELVILLE SHAVELSON

THE FIRST TIME I GOT SUED

I WAS IN London preparing to direct my screenplay of *Ike, The War Years*, a six-hour ABC miniseries on the World War II experiences of Gen. Dwight Eisenhower and his affair with his British driver, Kay Summersby, when the bomb went off. I got word from the network that Mamie Eisenhower was suing to prevent the film from being made. The network was closing down World War II and ordering me to retreat to Hollywood.

I had never before been sued by the wife of a president, and it hasn't happened again lately, so it may be of some interest to record the details here. In the Clinton era, it would be unthinkable for the wife of a president to sue anyone who had the temerity to suggest that her husband had been unfaithful only once.

The moment the purchase of Kay Summersby's book, *Past Forgetting,* had been announced by ABC, the pressures to stop the filming began. The venerable *New York Times,* close to the

Eisenhower family, denounced Kay's book as a prurient distortion of fact, a complete fabrication by Summersby, written only to make money. Why Kay would be interested in making money, when she knew she had only a little more than six months to live, the editorials never revealed. But they did call on ABC to stop preparing this insult to American history. Even though the truth had been vouched for by another, and trusted, president.

The full story had been revealed for the first time, even to Kay, by Harry Truman himself, the no-nonsense Give-'em-Hell president whom not even a network anchor would ever accuse of having had an orgasm in the Oval Office. In Truman's days in that office, the buck stopped there, and so did anything else that rhymed with it.

In 1973, in Harry Truman's oral history—not to be confused with Monica Lewinsky's—he told his biographer, Merle Miller, "Right after the war was over, Eisenhower wrote a letter to Gen. George Marshall, saying that he wanted to come back to the United States and divorce Mrs. Eisenhower, so he could marry this Englishwoman. Marshall wrote him back a letter the like of which I never did see. He said that if Eisenhower ever came close to doing such a thing, he'd not only bust him out of the Army, he'd see to it that not for the rest of his life would he be able to draw a peaceful breath. If ever again he even mentioned a thing like that, he'd see to it that the rest of his life was a living hell.

"One of the last things I did as president, I got those letters from his file in the Pentagon and I destroyed them."

With this testimony ignored, Kay, unlike Monica, never gave a serious blow to the presidency.

Kay Summersby wasn't that kind of girl. Beautifully Irish, emotionally British, in her late twenties when she was assigned to

drive the commander of Allied Forces even to the most dangerous battlefronts of World War II, she, like Monica, fell deeply in
love with one of the most powerful men in the world. And he
with her.

She never breathed a word of their affair until after Ike's
death, and refused to write about it in her memoirs until she
learned she herself was dying of cancer. She felt history demanded her story. History. Not, as in the case of Monica, the
National Enquirer.

Kay would never have made a deal to tell all just for a price, or
a guarantee of immunity. She had loved Ike. Deeply. When we attempted to tell this simple truth in that ABC Circle Films' miniseries in 1974, we were attacked by everyone in the press and also
the Eisenhower family.

It was Truman's revelation, Kay said, about Ike's letter to
General Marshall that she had never known existed, that made
her decide to write their love story, in the few months she had left
to live.

Kay died of cancer in 1974, shortly before the book appeared.

Just before its publication, Lou Rudolph, at that time one of
ABC's more intelligent production executives—in Lou's case, not
an oxymoron—sent me the galleys, and asked if I thought there
was a romantic movie in it.

I told him, "No."

What I saw in Kay's story was a chance to tell the history of
World War II on television, a war almost unknown to the Me
Generation. I felt it would hold them even through the deodor-
ant commercials because it could be structured around one of
the most unusual, least known, and most touching love stories I
had ever read.

Anticipating the network's fears, I told him I felt the Eisenhower family would want the story to be told, if only for history to recognize Ike as a human being, and forgive him for being one.

I soon lost my innocence. There is nothing, I soon learned, that people want to hear less than the truth. Especially about a national hero instead of a president who avoided his draft board.

Dwight Eisenhower never saw or mentioned Kay Summersby after that letter from General Marshall. Kay came to the United States after the war and tried to see him. She never did. There was no secretary in his outer office willing to help her. Or to take back the gifts Ike had given Kay, including the five-star pin and her American citizenship.

Kay Summersby died, alone, and, as she titled her memoirs, *Past Forgetting*. But the rest of the world did forget. Or, worse, refused to believe. Ike never had to swear anyone to secrecy by getting them a job. That was when a president could trust even the Secret Service.

It was a different world.

In the film, Kay says, "I know I'll be swept under the rug of American history. But I'll have a lot of distinguished company under that rug."

Little did she know she would one day be joined there by the leading citizen of Little Rock, Arkansas.

It's a very large rug.

Almost large enough for a whole network to hide under, I discovered. The first scene I wrote for the screenplay was the stormy meeting between Ike and Marshall over Ike's determination to marry Kay and divorce Mamie, based on the letters Truman had revealed. The rest of the movie was to flash back from there.

It flashed back right in my face. The network absolutely refused to allow me to mention any part of it. It didn't matter that it was true. The American public, as mentioned before, would not accept that kind of behavior from a national hero.

The network officials wanted me to meet with the Eisenhower family and assure them that all would be in good taste, emphasizing that we did not mean to demean Ike, but merely to present him as the man he really was, for the annals of history. Mamie herself would be allowed to read the finished script and lodge any objections, before the expensive shooting began.

I certainly didn't want to hurt a former first lady, who, like Hillary Clinton, never knew at first about her husband's affair.

I held several meetings with members of the Eisenhower family, hoping they would understand the importance of the historical truth. They didn't.

The United States Army, on the other hand, surprised me by offering me every cooperation, including access to all the combat footage shot by the Army in World War II, because the Army felt it was important to present a five-star general as human.

The network bravely insisted on continuing, despite the storm of disapproval that was appearing in the press almost daily. After a year of researching into the facts, I was firmly convinced that the seemingly dispassionate farm boy from Abilene, Kansas, and his beautiful but proper wartime driver from County Cork did indeed have a relationship that had an effect both on them and the greatest war in American history, and that no true record of that war could completely ignore it.

After finishing the screenplay, I went to London to scout locations.

And then Mamie's lawsuit was filed. Production was halted for

what became two long years, while the lawyers on both sides finished maneuvering. Finally, a truce was declared. The only stipula-
tion was that Mamie would be treated with respect. She certainly
deserved it and received it in the film, although I'm sorry she
didn't outlive her lawyers' case, and never saw the finished picture.

This is not the time or place to go into the rest of the stormy
adventures of shooting *Ike* on two continents, but eventually the
full six hours were filmed and—at least to me and the highly critical *New York Times*—received as, "Surprisingly absorbing drama.
The canvas covers all of Europe and parts of the military cam-
paign in North Africa. The key historical details are kept remark-
ably comprehensible. Lee Remick contributes one of her more
impressive performances. Robert Duvall is the indispensable
centerpiece of this production."

And, as Bill Clinton and Monica Lewinsky have both learned,
truth is almost impossible to destroy. The full truth about Kay
and Ike finally appeared in 1991, years after the movie was gone
and almost forgotten, from the same trustworthy *New York
Times* that had so strenuously attacked us almost twenty years
earlier. The *Times* news article read:

'INDEED A VERY DEAR FRIEND,'
Ike's Letters to Kay

By William Safire

In a Sotheby's catalogue for a sale in New York on June 13, I
found a historical love story in a collection of letters. The romance, its evidence now for sale to the highest bidder, was between Gen. Dwight Eisenhower and his secretary-driver, Kay
Summersby.

Rumors of the wartime relationship were denied at first by Ike's loyal friends . . . David Eisenhower, in his superb biography of his grandfather, noted that the truth "was only known by them, and both are gone."

It turns out the evidence is not gone. Thirty-seven lots of letters, documents and signed photographs from the estate of Kay Summersby are up for auction next week. . . . Nobody who reads these handwritten notes and letters from a caring, sensitive, gruff, sometimes distraught Eisenhower can easily say that Harry Truman was a liar. . . .

Eisenhower extricated himself because that was the path of duty and loyalty. She understood, steadfastly protected his secret until it could hurt nobody, then made it possible for their story—of four-star crossed lovers—to be appreciated by a later generation.

Perhaps Bill Clinton's legacy when he leaves office will include this credo:

"It is better to have loved and lost than never to have lied at all."

I still like Ike.

———————

Melville Shavelson claims he is a writer by choice, a producer through necessity, and a director in self-defense. He is also a playwright and the author of six published books.

He is a two-time Academy Award® nominee for his original screenplays, three times president of the Writers Guild of America, and recipient of its highest honor, the Laurel Award for Screenwriting. He is the current president emeritus of the Writers Guild Foundation.

He has an international record of hits he has filmed in the United States, England, Italy, France, and Israel, for Paramount, Warner Bros., United Artists, and, in television, NBC, ABC, and CBS.

APRIL SMITH

THE FIRST TIME I saw a four-wheel-drive vehicle was outside the executive building of a major studio. It was parked in a row of BMWs, the only one of its kind, certainly the only one with writing all over it. CHEROKEE CHIEF, it said, in big black letters, which was funny because it happened to belong to one of the chiefs of television, with whom I was about to take my first Hollywood meeting.

It was a golden day in late October 1977. I had arrived from Boston the afternoon before, having made the trip to Los Angeles at the urging of my friend and mentor, the writer Dan Wakefield, who had recently moved from Back Bay to West Hollywood.

"You have to come out here," he'd told me giddily on the phone. For what purpose, neither of us knew, but he was so exhilarated by the totally unexpected good fortune of having a series on the air that he surpassed his already legendary generosity, and put me up in a spectacular suite at the Chateau Marmont. Every day the manager would send fresh flowers, and at night I'd stand on the terrace in the exotic balmy air and watch helicopters sweep the grid with hot white searchlights. LAPD surveillance was unknown to me: I assumed the choppers were up there because someone was shooting a movie.

Here it was, Day Two, and already I was being swept into television.

We passed the enigmatic Cherokee Chief and walked into the Spanish-style building. I was more preoccupied with the stains on my pants suit than what it meant to be having a story meeting with a powerful studio executive. It was a summery blue cotton pants suit that had served me well in my day job as an advertising copywriter in Boston, but too thin for this cool fall day in southern California. I had come unprepared for any sort of business meeting, but it didn't matter. Although events were moving with the speed of light, everything seemed pleasantly haphazard and okay. In a screening room the day before, this executive had casually mentioned to Dan that he'd just sold a pilot to NBC-TV and was looking for a writer. The pilot concerned a boy who sails around the world in a sailboat. I had recently published a short story in the *Atlantic Monthly* about a family who sails around Long Island Sound. Close enough.

"I know the perfect writer," Dan had said. "She's arriving at LAX in an hour."

The Chief wanted to see me.

That a boy sailing around the world would be virtually unmakeable as a TV series, and that I had never written a screenplay nor even thought about writing one (I was a literary novelist-to-be with a pedigree from the Stanford Writing Center) seemed to be of no concern to anyone as we strolled into the office, a huge space designed to resemble the Anzo-Barrego Desert Preserve. There were cacti taller than humans and many valuable Native American artifacts. The executive was wearing jeans, a work shirt and cowboy boots. Until that moment, my working life had been about pitching print advertising campaigns to Yankee retailers in Brooks Brothers suits.

The executive liked my short story. "Have you ever written a screenplay?" he asked.

I said, "No."

"Do you think you could?"

I said, "Yes."

"Great," said the executive. "Take a shot at it."

"Let's go," said Dan.

We got up and left. As we walked down the steps into the sunshine I said, "Was that real?"

"Don't ask me," said Dan.

We went back to the cottage on Wetherly Drive he shared with his girlfriend and spent the rest of the afternoon staring into large globes of white wine and wondering at the mystery of the universe, when an agent appeared at the door. Dan, ever the thoughtful host, had asked his television agent to stop by because I now had a television assignment and was in need of one. Instantly, I had an agent. I moved out of the Chateau Marmont to Oakwood Garden Apartments in Marina Del Rey where I wrote the pilot (which was never made) and then several scripts for episodic shows produced by 20th Century-Fox before landing my first staff job.

A few weeks into my new life in Los Angeles, Dan and I were taking a walk on the beach. He led me out to the end of Venice

Pier. We looked back at the rows of funky beach houses, eccentric Rollerbladers and lazy afternoon strollers, the mountains to the north, and the misty metropolis with all its secrets, stretching out toward the desert.

"All this can be yours, said the devil," Dan joked, in a voice heavy with irony.

I took the deal.

On Christmas Day I found myself at a party in a condo on the very same beach. I was standing at the bottom of the stairs, near a telephone table, when the executive came up behind me, slipped both hands beneath my sweater, and over my breasts.

That was the first time I was felt up in Hollywood.

The executive was gone from the television business in a matter of seasons. Dan, fed up with the hypocrisy of it all, left also, to quit booze, remake his life, and discover the world of the spirit. I'm still here, sailing the bay, looking back at the shoreline.

————

April Smith is an Emmy-nominated writer/producer. She is also the author of the Los Angeles–based thrillers, *Be the One* and *North of Montana*, both published by Knopf.

ED SOLOMON

I WOULD HOVER in the back, silent and nervous. They would circle past in the darkness, eyes wide, staring. Gradually I'd make eye contact and they'd either lead me into a corner, or, if it was a club I knew well, I would take them to some secluded spot and we'd do it there. Usually I got twenty-five dollars, although there were some who'd pay more. If it was for a "session" I'd charge by the hour, and we'd often do those in my dorm. If my roommate was coming back, or if he was studying, I'd go to their place. I don't know how it led to where I am today, but if I were to be honest about how it began, really honest, I'd have to say it all started because of this girl, Lisa Bono, who never "liked me back."

In high school I had been funny for about twenty minutes. Actually, it was a little less than twenty minutes. And, to be honest, it was probably a little less than funny. It was the talent show, and my "talent" was stand-up comedy. I did jokes like *"I went to the sperm bank. It turns out there's a penalty for early withdrawal,"* and *"I went on a blind date. Well, it didn't start as a blind date, but when she saw me, she put her eyes out."* Okay, it was a *lot* less than funny. But I was seventeen. Lisa Bono, who sang "Send in the Clowns," came off the stage to wild applause. The other stand-up, Chet Urtses, the guy who used to show up to class with his underwear on the outside of his pants and who later in the year won "best sense of humor," did "fart impressions." And he did them well, apparently, 'cause not only did he get a standing ovation, but he went to the cast party with Lisa Bono. I went alone, and I sat on the floor with all the others listening to this guy Justin D'Arezzo sing "House at Pooh Corner." Again. In his most sensitive of falsettos. Heartbroken as I watched Chet and Lisa leave in the middle of that Joni Mitchell song about ponies going up and down, I figured the hell with it—clearly I don't have whatever *it* is that one's supposed to have to really succeed at this stuff—and I packed my comic aspirations into the closet with my high school yearbook. Three months later I left for UCLA to begin my *actual* life. My serious life. Pre-law, I was thinking. Or maybe business.

My mother drove me down on a Monday in September. While we were unloading the new clothes I would never wear and the color-tabbed binders I would never use, my roommate mentioned that the Comedy Store in Westwood was having open-mike night. I shrugged it off; I had to register the next morning. But two minutes after my mother left for Reseda to visit Aunt Ceil I was in line on Westwood Boulevard scratching out whatever jokes I could remember from the variety show. I watched with "professional" curiosity/jealousy the others in line ahead of me. There was a guy who spent his entire time slot shaving his leg. There was a woman who barked. There was someone who did something called "number humor." I don't remember the jokes, but one of the punch lines was "2, 4, 6, 8, 11."

I bounced onto the stage at 9:49, ignorant, innocent, and too clueless to be nervous. I did my opening joke, something about being in a porn film but quitting cause my part was too small. I remember being surprised at the first wave of laughter. And even more surprised at the second. It was like surfing in a sea of approval. And it was the fastest two minutes of my life (or, actually, the *second* fastest two minutes, but that's for a *different* "First Time" story). I floated off the stage at 9:51 with no sense of equilibrium and with the utter conviction that within weeks I'd be speaking directly to Lisa Bono from my new perch as permanent guest host of *The Tonight Show*.

I spent the next day only halfheartedly registering for classes. In fact, I took an extra-light load because I figured I'd be dropping out soon. I called everyone I knew from my hometown (there were 20 or so at UCLA at the time) and invited them to see me dazzle them the next Monday. I got business cards printed up. I styled my hair. I bought a sports coat.

The next week, fresh with eleven new jokes, a trendy, mullet-style Jew-fro, and an unworn, rolled-up-at-the-sleeves corduroy blazer, I got in line with the riffraff and polished my set on the back of a pee-chee. My friends arrived en masse at 8:00. At 11:48 I leapt onto the stage, confident and ebullient. At 11:50 I peeled myself off, morose and humiliated. It was the slowest two minutes of my life. For the entire 120 seconds—seconds which dripped by in sludgelike individual droplets—there had been abject, stone-cold radio silence. My mouth had dried halfway through and I did that thing where you swallow in the middle of your sentence. Twice. It was so bad that I felt more sorry for my friends than I did for myself—after all, they had to sit through it, and afterwards they were going to have to try and tell me it wasn't so bad. On the long walk back to the dorms, each took turns glancing at me sideways with the look of one who had just watched someone accidentally ejaculate while grooming a cat. No one even tried to lie and tell me it wasn't so bad. In fact, no one said anything. The next morning I added eight more units and dove into what was to be a year of pretty serious study. I became an econ major. And I vowed I would never go back to the Comedy Store. Ever.

Then Lisa Bono called.

It was November of the next year. She was in town with her parents to check out UCLA (she was thinking of transferring). She wanted to know if I'd take her on a tour of the campus (yes), and if I wanted to go with them to the Comedy Store that night (no, well, okay, yes). Gulp. I don't know what I was more nervous about: seeing Lisa, or going back to a place where I was certain I would be not just unwelcome, but ridiculed. Of course no one even vaguely remembered me. I was, thankfully, gloriously unfamous. I was just an anonymous guy with a two-drink minimum sitting in the darkness. And I was watching professional comedians at work for the first time. Really watching them. Studying them, actually. And after about an hour or so I found myself up and away from the table and wandering toward the back of the room.

There were comedians everywhere. The more my eyes adjusted, the more seemed to appear. There were at least a dozen comics hanging by the bar. There were six hovering near the kitchen. Two more were standing, hands in pockets, by the entrance. They were all watching, judging, smirking, wishing their friends would bomb (but not enough to deaden the crowd for them). Of course at the time I wasn't aware of the many variations on the complex inner workings of the mind of a comic. To me, at that moment, I was in some sort of strange fantasy. I was surrounded by people who were funny for a living.

And then I saw *him*. The most famous person I'd ever seen up close. The guy from *Good Times*. The Dyn-O-Mite Guy. Alone against the back wall. Just *standing there*.

Then he looked at me. And I looked at him. And I felt so young and small and he seemed so . . . famous. And, somehow, I found myself inching myself closer to him. Finally, when I got so close I either had to kiss him or speak, I stuttered out, "Um, excuse me, Mr. Walker, sir, are you . . . do you ever . . . do you ever need writers?"

"Son, we *always* lookin' for writers." He literally rubbed me on the top of my head. "Dean."

Instantly another man was standing next to me.

"Take this fine specimen of a man upstairs."

I gulped, and followed Dean.

The room was red and dim and smelled of sweat and marijuana. I sat on the lip of a naugahyde couch beneath a wall of wittily signed head shots. Muted laughter came from below where Lisa Bono sat with her parents and my empty chair. Dean straddled a stool across from me, his leg bouncing rapidly, his head cocked and steady, his eyes suspicious.

"So . . . what do you got?"

I considered fleeing. Or crying. Instead, I just cleared my throat, took a deep breath.

I tried computer dating. I said I wanted someone who liked to

wake at dawn and go for long walks in the rain. They sent me a
Marine Corps drill instructor.

Dean stared at me, his leg firing away.

I just took my driver's test. I'm trying to figure out if it was the
pedestrian I hit which took the points off, or the fact that I hit him
in his living room.

My girlfriend has what you'd call Early American features. It
means she looks like a buff—

"Hang on." Dean stood. "Don't go anywhere."

He walked out. I glanced up at the black-and-white photos
on the wall. Pictures taken in the late seventies, full of big hair,
big grins, and promise. The door creaked open.

"Hey." A rather large guy entered, nodding as he looked
around and immediately closed the door behind him. He was di-
sheveled, and had the furtive, darting eyes of the vaguely desperate. He sat right next to me and leaned in conspiratorially. "So,
uh . . . you writing for Jimmie?"

I didn't know.

"Listen," he moved even closer, "I don't know what your guy's
deal is, but, like, I got, I don't know, forty bucks, no, forty-f—"

The door opened again. The other guy turned quickly. Dean
glared at him. "Beat it, fat-ass."

"Hey, I can—"

"Mike, I'm tellin' ya."

The other guy, Mike, scurried off.

"Loser." Dean shook his head, then reached into his pocket
and pulled out a wad of bills.

"Here's the deal. Write 'em up, give 'em to me, he'll try 'em
out. If they work, it's twenty-five a joke. You got 'em written
down? Typed up or anything?"

I shook my head.

"Aright, fine, hang on, you got a pen? Lemme borrow a piece of paper. What was the one, the car one, the pedestrian one?"

I told him. He wrote it down on my valet parking check.

"Here's twenty-five bucks. It's for the car one, or a different one, if that doesn't work. Consider it a deposit. Write up the rest, bring 'em back tomorrow. Where do you live?"

"UCLA. The dorms. Sproul Hall."

"What's your number?"

I told him. He wrote it down, then disappeared again. I waited a while, but he never returned. So I wandered back down to the main room and retook my seat by the Bonos just as the Dyn-O-Mite Guy was going up onto the stage. I started to try and tell them about what had happened, but they were so excited to see the Dyn-O-Mite Guy that they didn't want to hear it. Then something really odd happened. About ten minutes into his set, the Dyn-O-Mite Guy pulled out a small piece of paper. It was my valet parking check. He glanced at it, then glanced right back up at the audience. And he told my joke. The car joke, the pedestrian thing. And before I could even realize what had happened I was looking around at the people laughing. A Professional Famous Person had just said something I had written. I glanced over at Lisa Bono. She was looking at me with a cocked eyebrow and smiling. Then she started wagging her finger at me.

"Hey," she beamed knowingly, "that's the joke you did at the variety show."

I nodded, proud.

"So *that's* where you got it."

I started to try and explain, but the people in front of us were already *shushing* us. When I reapproached it in the car on the way home, they actually didn't believe me. Strangely, with a surge of quiet confidence I have yet to feel again, I let it drop.

For what it's worth:

Lisa Bono is apparently still unmarried. I haven't spoken to her since that night.

The Dyn-O-Mite Guy still does stand-up. He did that pedestrian joke as recently as 1990, on a Showtime special.

The fat guy, Mike (not his real name), lost 65 pounds and now stars on a very successful sitcom.

Chet Urtses is the bartender/entertainment director on a cruise ship.

Ed Solomon's feature screenwriting credits include *Men in Black, Bill and Ted's Excellent Adventure, Bill and Ted's Bogus Journey,* and *Leaving Normal.* He began his career as a playwright, joke writer, and stand-up comedian, and wrote for Fox TV's *It's Garry Shandling's Show* for three seasons. He lives in Santa Monica, California, with his wife, Cynthia, and their son, Evan.

BETH SULLIVAN

THE FIRST TIME I truly understood the love/hate relationship that the television business has with its viewers was in a testing session of an episode of *Dr. Quinn, Medicine Woman.* For anyone who has not experienced spying on a "focus group," it consists of network representatives and the producers of a show sitting behind a two-way mirror and observing a roomful of people ("J. Q. Public") watch, rate and then discuss their opinions of the show just screened for them. It has a creepy, "big brother" feel to it, despite knowing that the viewers, their name cards in front of them, are entirely aware of your presence on the other side of the mirror.

In one of these sessions, an all-male group was viewing a particularly serious, particularly female-themed episode in which Dr. Quinn herself miscarries a child and, in the absence of Sully, tries to carry the burden of the loss alone, finally realizing that she must turn to others for help. (An Old West debunking of the "Superwoman" myth.) Anyway, I found myself putting my feet up and saying, "These guys are going to *hate* this." Sure enough, I thought, look at all the shifting in their seats, the casual getting up to get a beverage. One guy must have gotten up three times to pour himself some more coffee, his back to the screen. I glanced down at the profile sheet to see who he was. "Mike," a carpenter by trade. To my utter shame forever, I (from working-class families on both sides) made the smart-assed prediction that "Mike" is going to give us a "0." He probably didn't make it to algebra, so at least we're safe from negative numbers.

The episode ended, and the moderator asked the men to write on their cards how they'd rate the episode and to display them. The moderator always starts with the highest rating and asks what the person liked, etc. to get the discussion rolling and to embolden those who disagree to formulate their thoughts. Well, to my shock and amazement "Mike" had put a big fat "10" next to his name card, the only member of the group to do so, the others averaging a still surprising "7"–"8". But "10" from *Mike?* "So, Mike," the moderator began, "you really liked the show. What did you like about it?" Mike took a sip of coffee, choosing his words, then said quietly, matter-of-factly, "I like that it makes you think and feel deeply about things that are important." I was stunned and humbled and also appalled that I had let myself get caught up in that facile Hollywood disdain for the audience in an effort to protect my feelings from being hurt by the criticism I expected. It was the first time I was forced to realize that, perhaps, all those other people in the business, whom *I* criticize for underestimating the audience, might actually be doing so for precisely the same simple emotional reason—to protect *their* feelings from being hurt.

Okay, okay, enough psychology and compassion. Back to the point. Ethically speaking, those "unwashed masses," those "people we fly over," are the hardworking, deep-feeling people who make this country run. They must *never* be underestimated. Most of us in this business are but a measure away in talent or hustle from precisely who "they" are. We may afford different restaurants, clothes and cars, but we all eat, get dressed and drive to work. We all talk about the same economy, the same Saddam Hussein, and the same president's cigar proclivities. And most of us get our news from our local paper, *Time* magazine and CNN. The culture of information has a common denominator unequaled in history, due to retail homogenization, mass media and the Internet. "They," in fact, are a diverse, complex and, yes, sophisticated audience that deserves to be heard and responded to.

Pragmatically speaking, it's just plain bad business to underestimate the American television audience. It leads to second-guessing what "they" want, when they're more than willing to tell you. It's even worse business to jump on the bandwagon of every passing theory of commercial sponsorship as to *who* the audience *really* is. The latest theory from the whiz kids of the Madison Avenue ad agencies is that the only viewers truly susceptible to having their buying habits influenced are young, urban males. (Well, they have to tell their clients *something* to justify their link in the food chain.) The reality, of course, is that aiming programming only at young urban males (even if the theory was valid) is to alienate the vast majority of Americans turning on their television sets and trying to find something that speaks to *their* hearts and minds. In such a sprawling and diverse population as the United States, this seems like such common sense that one wonders why it even needs to be stated. However, one look at the disastrous fatality rate of new shows each season makes one think it should be shouted from every window. American viewers are "mad as hell" and they've proved they're "not going to take it anymore."

In the last decade alone, the networks have lost another 33 percent of their former viewers. Nothing seems to be being learned, because everything is being dealt with at the development and programming levels rather than listening and responding to the very audience sought after. There's a lot of hoopla made over testing and Nielsens, but there's not much stock put in their results. Network execs have mixed feelings, to say the least, about testing, because of the shows that wind up contradicting the predictions. No responsibility is ever taken for how those shows are publicized, promoted or placed (or even worse, moved around) on the schedule. And the Nielsen ratings are praised or damned, depending on whether the numbers are favorable to the show in question. (A better means of measuring the viewing habits of one hundred million people is needed, and the Nielsens are rightly under fire as they face the Y2K.)

However, there are plenty of other sources from which to derive a more accurate concept of what viewers want. A recent Temple University study, commissioned by SAG, documented how dismally prime-time television underrepresents and misrepresents huge segments of the population, including women, Hispanics, Asian-Pacific and Native Americans, the disabled and seniors (that now includes anyone over 49). To paraphrase former SAG president Richard Masur, there's a large gap between the fictional world created for television and the real-world audience that watches those fictional creations.

How many "flukes," such as *Murder, She Wrote, Doctor Quinn,*

Medicine Woman, Ally McBeal or *Providence* do there have to be before networks stop making pronouncements about the viability of "single female lead" series? The same goes for any other category, such as pronouncing sitcoms dead . . . until they weren't, until a quality show (Cosby) came along that touched the audience beyond the level of phony laugh tracks. Then drama was dead . . . until it wasn't. (Even Saturday night was dead . . . until it wasn't.) When will programming be based purely on the quality of a series? And when will one of the main criteria for quality be to "think and feel deeply about things that are important"? Because that's what the American audience wants.

Beth Sullivan, the creator and executive producer of the hit television series *Dr. Quinn, Medicine Woman,* is a past member of the Writers Guild of America, west, Board of Directors and a former trustee of the Writers Guild Foundation.

ROBIN SWICORD

DADA LA-LA

My FIRST screenplay was called *Stock Cars for Christ*. Inexplicably, my agent Merrily Kane sold it. MGM sent an unnecessarily long car around to take me to the airport for a story meeting in L.A. I was buoyant with the joy of finally getting to make a movie, and relieved to be no longer strictly poor. I spent the flight from New York wondering if the studio would really go along with the title. *Stock Cars for Christ* was a comedy about facing down personal demons and becoming your own hero. In the first two pages of *Stock Cars for Christ*, a hapless young man named Ulysee Glover does a driving stunt that sends his car flying off a bridge in Panama City Beach, Florida. His car lands on a water-ski platform, accidentally flattening a bevy of southern bathing beauties who are posing for a postcard. When I arrived at the story meeting, the producer said, "I love the title." I thanked him, wondering how soon we would begin filming.

"Fantastic opening!" he went on. I made a private note to ask him later who the studio had in mind for Ulysee. "But we have to change it. It's too unsympathetic. The way we see it, Ulysee's car doesn't land on the girls."

I realized, chagrined, that I had been disgracefully unclear in my writing. I explained apologetically, "It isn't gory, it's more comic—the setup of the bathing beauties, the car in the air and the boy's reaction as he realizes too late that the girls are there." "We have to change it," the producer repeated. He put forth his idea. "The car lands in the water, missing the girls. It only scares them." I silently cursed myself for not writing clearly enough for people to understand. "I'm sorry," I said, "but if Ulysee doesn't flatten them, he has nothing to feel guilty about. He goes to jail, and when he emerges he has lost his sense of himself. It's the enormity of his crime that causes him to give up his boyhood dream of stunt driving—that's what launches the story." "He can't go to jail," the producer explained patiently. "We don't want our hero to be some criminal." "He's not really a criminal," I said, wondering what was wrong with me that I couldn't make such a simple point clear. "He's just a kid who makes a mistake. It has to be a big enough mistake that Ulysee backs away from his talent and transfers his ambition to helping Sonny True become a great driver again." The story editor and the producer exchanged a look. "Well, maybe the kid can spend one night in the county jail," the producer said, in the spirit of compromise. "For scaring the girls. Then we see a shot of him hitchhiking out of town." I made a mental note to go over this later with the director, who would be hired any moment, I presumed.

The producer and the story editor turned to page five. "This Sonny True guy," the producer went on, pensively, "he's not really a born-again Christian, is he?" I quelled a pang of self-loathing at my utter inability to write with any clarity whatsoever. "He's definitely born again." I said. "Page eight? His stock car bursts into flames? He's burned from head to toe, and page nine he has a hospital bed conversion. That's what makes him start putting on this Passion Play with stock cars." "Sonny's not disfigured, is he?" the producer asked, with a note of dismay. "He's scarred," I verified, uncertainly. "That's why he feels like a freak." "We can change that," the producer said, comfortingly. "We don't want him to be unsympathetic."

Ten months and nine drafts later, I ran into David Chasman, former head of United Artists, who was then a senior executive at MGM. "How's *Stock Cars*?" he asked, jovially. I admitted that I felt a little confused. "I hope I can get the script right," I said, "so y'all will finally make the movie." It was then that I got my first and maybe only piece of good advice ever on writing movies. "Your getting the script right doesn't mean the movie will be made," Chasman assured me. "Movies go into production all the time with perfectly terrible scripts. Movies get a green light for a lot of reasons, but our having a good script is rarely one of them." That's when I understood that I didn't understand anything at all. It was fantastically liberating.

Robin Swicord is the writer of *Practical Magic, Little Women, Mathilda* (with her husband, Nicholas Kazan), *The Perez Family,* and *Shag.*

MIGUEL TEJADA-FLORES

THE FIRST TIME I used a Macintosh computer, I had no idea it would change my life so radically. It was some years ago, in the mid–1980s. At the time, I was writing a project whose protagonists took an extended trip from Washington, D.C., down through the South; since I'd never really been to either D.C. or the South, I'd convinced my producers to cough up enough travel and research expenses to allow myself and my writing partner to make the same trip that our main characters were going to take. I'd flown to D.C., rented a car, and found myself staying with friends of friends, who lived in an old rambling farmhouse somewhere in the Maryland countryside. During the days, my partner and I put in long hours in D.C., wandering the halls of power, talking with movers and shakers and soaking up as much atmosphere as we could stand; but evenings were reserved for dinners, philosophizing, making extensive notes on

the characters for our script-in-progress . . . and plain old veg-
ging out . . . before seeking solace in Morpheus's embrace. I really
hadn't planned on staying up until three in the morning playing
with this weird and cool machine I stumbled across . . . but life is
full of surprises.

The operative word here is "playing." The inner technical
complexities of the Macintosh computer (the original old square
boxy Mac with a relatively small built-in screen) which I discovered in the farmhouse were far beyond me . . . but somehow, the-
oretical and technical considerations didn't seem to matter: It
only took a few seconds to figure out that there was this cool little pointer thingie which I could move around on the screen with
this weird doohickus called a mouse . . . and that when I clicked
it on certain pictures, or "icons," then even more cool things
might happen. The process was satisfyingly addictive, and the
more I fooled around, the more the hours whiled themselves
away until I finally came to my senses and realized it was time to
stop playing with the damn thing and get to bed before the sun
came up. But even after I'd stopped playing with it, I couldn't
stop remembering what fun it had been . . .

"Fun" is not a word I would have used to describe working on
a computer. I'd used a few computers before; in fact, I'd even
owned two, acquired a year or two earlier, whose intricate command structure I had devoted some time to mastering, on the
general theory that, as a writer, having a computer would somehow make things "easier" and more productive. And I'd almost
convinced myself that it was true. My first computers hadn't
been totally without merit. They'd finally freed me from the
drudgery of having to type and retype my screenplay drafts over
and over and over, until they were as perfect as I could get them.

(A habit developed both because of financial constraints, in leaner years, when I couldn't afford either typist or typing service . . . and also out of creative paranoia: I'd had a few experiences where so-called experienced typists had changed or altered some of my punctuation, line spacing, and even a few words . . . and I simply didn't trust anyone else to type my words out as well as I could.) My first, crude computers did a nice job of printing out the words I'd typed into my "files"; later, during rewrites, I had discovered the luxury of "saving" alternate versions or drafts. So, I knew there were definite, practical advantages to writing on a computer, advantages which I could not only appreciate (the rational, objective side of me) . . . but also feel proud of (the irrational, subjective "inner writer"). And now we get to the crux of the matter: "feeling proud of oneself." Because, let's face it, in the infancy of personal computers, writers didn't have a lot of choices. There were a handful of so-called word-processing programs, and the one thing they all had in common was: Their myriad complexities were extremely difficult to learn, let alone master. It took a real effort of will to sit down and memorize all of the scores of keystrokes, the commands, the file structure/s, and the not-so-joyous endless battles fought, on a daily basis, while attempting to Save, Open or Delete documents . . . without somehow accidentally "trashing" everything one had done. Printing out "hard copy" (paper copies as opposed to the purer, cyberspace files where words seemed to reside in a pleasing electronic void) was often a daunting task, involving prayer, threats, muttered imprecations, and desperate phone calls to pals who were more technologically inclined than you happened to be. Let's face it: To use those early generations of computers . . . you had to be a genuine card-carrying Nerd. Time for a little True

Confession here: Not only had my writing partner and I received our *first* writing credit on *Revenge of the Nerds* (a shared story credit) . . . but, going further back, into the dim prehistory of my teenage life . . . I had been a serious and genuine Nerd for as long as I could remember. (Some people think it's a state of mind. Some people think it's a way of life. They may be right.) And the thing about being a Nerd is . . . when you do stuff which is hard, and challenging, and taxes your brain cells . . . part of you likes to *boast* about it. Back in those early, primordial days, if you examined the relative handful of writers and screenwriters who'd mastered the technical and intellectual complexities of computer use . . . the truth is, many of us were more inordinately proud of our accomplishments. It gave us something to crow about, an "edge," and like quite a few of my writing colleagues, I was guilty of the sin of pride in those days. I liked the feeling that I'd been able to master a challenging new form of technology and use it in my creative labors; the fact that most of the software in that early epoch (everything from writing programs to operating systems) was ridiculously complicated was an additional feather in our caps. But the truth of the matter is, no matter what we told other people . . . it was never really "fun."

But that night, sitting up at three in the morning in a nineteenth-century farmhouse somewhere in Maryland, and staring at this strange little Macintosh computer with its built-in screen and its mouse, there was no denying the fact: I was having fun. I could take my words and play with them in new ways. I could change the way they looked—giving them different fonts, different typefaces, different styles and sizes—and I could do it all in "realtime," and look at it right there on the screen in front of me. Today, in 1999, as we're all counting down the months and weeks and hours to the new millennium, it's hard to remember that, way back when, computers *couldn't* do stuff like this. They *couldn't* show you, on a screen, *exactly* what you were doing (or wanted to do), *exactly* the way you wanted it to look. Today we casually chat about graphics accelerators and 3-D chips and color printers whose realism rivals that of high-density glossy photographs. But fifteen-odd years ago, it was a different story. In those relatively Dark Ages, writers who used computers had dark screens with glowing green or yellow letters and a blinking cursor. If you wanted to edit words, or change their appearance, or do just about anything, you had to know the correct command or sequence of commands and keystrokes . . . and heaven help you if you got just *one* of those keystrokes wrong. That was the Brave New World which we had all gotten used to, and which we exuberantly proclaimed, in the same manner as Voltaire's "Candide," that it Surely Must Be the Best of All Possible Worlds. But, truth be told: It wasn't. And that night, sitting there with the remains of an idiotic grin on my face, trying to figure out just why I'd spent the last four hours playing with some silly machine . . . I *realized*. That, no matter what else it was capable of, this funny, boxy-looking little Macintosh computer could do something that no other high-tech machine I'd ever worked on could . . .

It could make the process bloody enjoyable. It could turn drudgery into a game. It could turn a serious, focused, rational process . . . into a lot of silly and irrational fun.

The rest, as they say, is a long story . . . and, in my case, an ongoing one. I went out and bought a Mac and started writing on it. Then, to my surprise, I started using it to do other things than "just" writing. A lot of other things. Like organizing . . . not just plot points and outlines . . . but information . . . and ideas. One thing led to another . . . just as, in life, one script follows another . . . we evolve as writers, as human beings . . . and the games we play also evolve. As do the machines we play them on. Today, as I write these words, I've "evolved" through half a dozen newer, more advanced Macs (or "computers" as some folks like to call them). My newest is a high-speed model with a mammoth storage drive, a dedicated backup system, a color monitor which shows me an entire page of the script I'm writing, and enough bells and whistles to make just about anyone deliriously happy. But, most importantly of all, it's still fun to use. I've sometimes wondered if having a writing tool which encourages me to play games . . . also influences the writing games I play. The answer to this question, of course, is a resounding Yes . . . No . . . and Maybe. And, every once in a blue moon, a memory comes to me—of that fateful night . . . when my life, as a screenwriter, was irrevocably changed . . . altered by a phenomenon so profoundly subtle that I nearly didn't realize, at the time it was happening, that anything had happened.

But it did happen. And it—the moment . . . the computer . . . the process . . . the fact that I was "having fun" . . . and the additional fact that, in a strange half-perceived instant of awareness, I *realized* it—"it" definitely changed my life.

(I know, I know, I can hear the naysayers out there already. You know them, our venerable brothers and sisters who tell us, almost always with serious and sincere countenances, that the only *real* way to write . . . is with a quill pen, on papyrus . . . and either with inks you've ground yourself or, better yet, your own blood. Anything else isn't real writing. Those true purists may occasionally use legal pads and pencils . . . and now and again you may find one of them secretly pecking away on a typewriter, preferably an old manual Royal or Underwood . . . but if no one's looking, maybe even a later-model IBM Selectric. But they all draw the line when it comes to mixing computers and the creative writing process. East is East, they tell us, and West is West, and never the twain shall meet. Nor shall any "real" writing ever be done on one of those newfangled thingummies. The more they rant and rave, the more I smile, secretly, to myself.)

But enough already. Time, as they say, is a' wastin', and I'm afraid, as always, I've got work to do. Some of the drudgery which my so-called fun machine imposes on me from time to time. I have to do a backup. I should probably defragment my hard disk. I need to copy some essential files onto my PowerBook (which some people persist in calling a laptop). All worthy activities, which, alas, must be done on a regular basis if our computers—and our lives—are going to operate efficiently. Which, strangely, brings me to my next subject, the real thing I wanted to talk about: Have you ever wondered how it is that some people are so incredibly efficient and organized . . . while others (I'm not naming names) seem so . . . disorganized? Is it simply a clash between learned behaviors, as the sociologists would have us believe? Or are we cursed and/or blessed at birth by genetic differences which we can never alter (not this century, at least) . . . no matter how neat or disorderly we struggle to be/not be? And what, you may be asking yourselves, does any (or all) of this have to do with writing . . . or computers? The answer's really quite simple . . . if you think about it. But I'm afraid that, once again, I've run out of space, not to mention time. So let's do this the simple way: Have your computer . . . ask my computer*. . . and maybe then we can get some serious communication going here.

Miguel Tejada-Flores lives in Talent, Oregon, in a house that was built in 1902 and still doesn't have central heating; although he enjoys ranting and raving about the benefits of technology, he still has to go out and split firewood with a maul . . . if he doesn't want to freeze to death while sitting in front of his Mac . . . a place you can often find him. And if your computer wants to talk to his computer, you can reach it—and him—at his e-mail address: MiguelATF@aol.com.

*Fifteen-odd years ago, one computer talking to another computer was a complex and arcane process, attempted only by the most hardy and dedicated techno-dweebs. Today, with the ubiquitous blossoming of what we call e-mail . . . it seems hard to imagine, that, once upon a time . . . this burgeoning form of cyber-netic/epistolary communication . . . was a rare and arcane art, reserved for the high priests and initiates of the movement.

JOAN TEWKESBURY

IN PRAISE OF THE PAUSE

GOOD DIALOGUE is a miracle. Smart-mouth dialogue, funny dialogue, important idea dialogue . . . words rattling along at a rapid clip, pushing through the silence, but as a writer, I'm really in love with good pauses. The tension between words where unadorned truth resides. That time just before the kiss, the punch, the hello, the good-bye, the "Oh I get it." Time breathlessly suspended, like you might just die waiting in the pause before action.

The first time a good pause presented itself on my page was in a stark motel room in Jackson, Mississippi. An added scene was required in a few hours and no words would come. Writer's block obviously. The characters simply refused to talk.

She in the dressing table mirror. He, behind it. She caught up in her pin curls and hairbrush hoping for beautiful so he would love her. He hoping he won't get caught for bank robbery, not seeing beauty or anything else, only wanting to disappear.

"You love me don't you, Bowie?" Then nothing . . . not one word, just silence. I tried again.

"I help you don't I, Bowie?" in a whining, compliant tone, only this time she leaned around the dressing table mirror, tried to find him, couldn't. He was hiding, pulled back into the shadows to dream about escape, playing baseball, a life on the road, money . . . it was 1935, the Depression, he was poor.

After a half an hour of hopeful anticipation for the perfect combination of words to create a sentence of light and funny or profundity and weight . . . "Sure," was the only word that appeared on the page.

Certainly there would be more. I waited. Nothing happened. I prepared myself for the worst. Then, I looked again. Time had strung itself out, become a clothesline for honest-to-God truth in the lapse. They'd seen each other in the mirror. Their accidental reflected glimpse caught them, gave away what they were too afraid to say. She was desperate and he was haunted. Ultimately the two actors pushed the length of that pause, dragged out the discomfort of revelation, and the perfect blend of nothing and everything stayed on and on like bad weather.

Now these words and pauses were not momentous like Pinter or Stoppard or Mamet, but they were correct. The characters had addressed the dilemma but only after the writer had grown weary with the puzzle and stepped out of the way.

Spaces, silence, gaps, word intermissions filled with behavior . . . Perhaps it's the collaboration with chance that pleases me most, the uncertainty of how the actor will maneuver time, but it delights and fascinates, holds all sorts of danger and promise.

So . . . a toast to the stark motel room in Mississippi where I learned to trust the quiet and the characters in pursuit of communication . . . whatever the form.

––––––––––

Joan Tewkesbury is the writer of *Nashville,* writer/director of *Cold Sassy Tree,* and most recently writer/director/choreographer of *Dance Card* for the Oregon Ballet Theatre and the playwright of *Jammed* for Frances Fisher performed at the Edinburgh Festival.

CAROLINE THOMPSON

THE FIRST TIME I got paid for writing a movie was also the first time I had a studio deal. I would rather not name the studio or that studio's then-players—not because those players are playing anymore, but because I hate hurting anyone's feelings—even those of former studio executives—even if it is oxymoronic to mention "feelings" and "studio executives" in the same sentence. Where, by the way, do studio executives go when they leave their jobs? They have everyone in town, kowtowing and quaking one day, then the next, poof, they've vanished, as if they'd never existed. Are they all hiding out together on the same Pacific island? What do they DO there? What do they talk about?

The movie was a horror movie pretentiously called *Distant Music*. I'm embarrassed to recall the passion I dedicated to safeguarding my impression of myself as a serious writer. In this case, I had even gone so far as to take the title phrase from James

Joyce's short story "The Dead." How could I be selling out if I were quoting Joyce? I don't remember, but I can picture myself assuring my friends that I was working on a script whose title had come from Joyce. It's probably all I told them about the project. We didn't say "project" then, I think. What did we say? Does the concept of "selling out" even exist anymore? I wonder when I last heard anyone fret about it. It seems to me that today if people could, people would be dying to "sell out." "Buy it! Buy it! Oh, please, for God's sake, won't you buy it?!" Lord, this makes me sound so old. I'm not. I swear!

I spent weeks with a young producer, concocting the story of *Distant Music*. He was barely twenty-one, but had the affect of someone far older. It helped that he was British, that he had an old man's wart on his nose, that he was the son of a famous actor and that he had a well-cultivated world-weariness. I was determined, but shy and insecure about my abilities, and so I let the young producer send me off again and again to refine the idea. Every time I returned to pitch the changes to him (that word was already in use), I had a terrible hollow feeling in my gut. I'm certain he enjoyed the power—he had at his tender age perfected the dead-eye stare while "listening." At the end of any given pitch, he would sigh and ruminate, then take a deep breath and pontificate at length. I have to admit that I enjoyed it too at first—it was attention I hadn't yet gotten—but I tired of it pretty soon.

Eventually, we took *Distant Music* on the road. To this day, pitching leaves me hollow and sweaty, so I can only imagine the froth I got into then. But the mind is a beautiful thing—mine protects me from all sorts of shocks and unpleasant memories, so I can't recall much about our experience. I should call the young producer—now a middle-aged agent, though, at last sighting,

looking no older than when he was theoretically young—and ask
him if he remembers where and to whom we went. Was it five studios or ten or only just the one that bought it? But I won't call
him—why talk to more agents than I have to? I also won't call him
because it doesn't matter.

Sooner or later, a young executive—now head of television at
another studio—wanted to buy *Distant Music*. Hurray! Money!
An office on the lot!—my first and last, but then very important
to me as a sign of my new status as a successful screenwriter.
Never mind that I lived on the other side of the hill, meaning an
hour or more away in traffic, and that my office had no light, was
subterranean, was, in fact, in the BASEMENT of a parking structure. What did I care? It was still the magical OFFICE ON THE
STUDIO LOT. But, I'm getting ahead of myself. Even though the
executive said yes, I did not yet have a deal. At this particular studio, the executives functioned as glorified clearinghouses. They
did not have the power to okay a development deal. Here, a
writer had to pitch to the HEAD OF THE STUDIO.

Entering the head of the studio's office, the young producer
held the door for me. He had manners because of being British, I
think. Otherwise, there are no manners, i.e., no thinking of anyone else before thinking of oneself, in Hollywood. My heart
throbbed. My throat dried up. My hands shook. I was dying for a
cigarette but glad it wasn't appropriate to smoke (you could still
smoke in buildings then) because I didn't want them to see my
hands shake. THEM was indeed the operative word. In that
room, in a circle of chairs sat the HEAD OF PRODUCTION
AND HIS ENTIRE PRODUCTION STAFF. God knows how
many executives plus the boss. The head of production looked
like one of my dad's golf partners—he seemed tired and faintly

bemused at finding himself here, surrounded by his staff, especially the adoring young female executive on his right, reputed to be his mistress and, indeed, she did glower at me, the only other female in the room, and kind of turn and hover over him in what I could only take to be a gesture of territoriality. The young producer gave me an embarrassingly glowing and very flowery introduction, then, with a sweep of the arm, he left me hanging.

Later, in the elevator, he said he felt sorry for me on account of the obvious dry mouth and my voice trembling. The actual telling of the story gapes like the blackness one sees just before fainting. I was terrified. I remember nothing. Except for the beaming face of head of production (I swear there were cleats on the bottom of his shoes) when I finished telling the tale.

"Wonderful! Engaging! Fascinating!" he crowed. "But couldn't you include satanic ritual? Couldn't you actually make it ABOUT satanic ritual?"

Satanic ritual had nothing to do with the story. Nothing at all.

"Of course, we could!" bellowed young producer goodnaturedly. "That's brilliant! Much better than our original concept."

Couldn't we make WHAT about satanic ritual? How did that fit in? What in the world was he talking about? These were the questions inside my head. They did not, in that room, find their way out of my mouth. Instead, I stood there shaking hands with the head of production and each of his now-smiling minions. They were congratulating me and welcoming me into the studio family.

Within the week, I found myself in the coveted, subterranean office, staring at my blank computer screen, reading books devoted to the satanic, scaring myself so badly I could hardly sleep. Believing that thoughts are things, I spun myself into a tizzy over inviting the dark forces into my consciousness and the world. At the same time, I was thrilled to be here and very anxious to do well . . . but I had absolutely no idea at all of what I was supposed to be doing. Not a clue in the world.

———————

Caroline Thompson is the author of such screenplays as *Edward Scissorhands, The Nightmare Before Christmas,* and *The Secret Garden.* There was a happy moment when the writing and directing of *Black Beauty* made her beloved of twelve-year-old girls everywhere.

PETER TOLAN

I REMEMBER vividly the first time I knew I was going to be a writer. I was sixteen years old and had not written anything of substance other than book reports, thank-you cards and weekly Saturday night notes to my parents promising that this time I'd definitely be home before midnight and not to wait up. But there was a specific moment when, without a particle of doubt, I knew I would be a writer.

My first exposure to the writer's life was *The Dick Van Dyke Show*, and I spent countless afternoons watching it as a child of no more than seven or eight. We had a round, worn, white hassock, and I would turn it on its side and drape myself over it, then slowly rock back and forth as I watched the show and dreamed about having a job where I could laugh all day and tell jokes and then go home to Mary Tyler Moore and maybe get to see her in her underwear. (Again, I was seven or eight. Seeing a girl in her underwear was my life's ambition.) Maybe it was because the show was so wonderfully funny, or perhaps it was just the hassock pressing against my sensitive boy parts, but those afternoons helped define who I was and who I would become. But this was not the moment when I knew I would be a writer.

Ten years later I was in high school. My luck with the distaff gender was such that the time I had spent with the hassock still counted as my most meaningful sexual relationship. The truth was I had no interest in girls. I'd found a different passion, a flaming temptress that consumed me night and day, and her name was The Theater. How I pitied my classmates as I watched them shuffling through the halls between classes, the fire behind their eyes completely doused. They had no idea what their future would be, whereas I was unqualifiedly certain of my path and destiny. I would conquer Broadway within a matter of weeks after graduating. I would be working with the cream of the theater crop. I could even imagine a show being written for me by the likes of Comden and Green. (Never mind that I had once thought they were one person, a certain Comden N. Green. This could be excused. I was fifteen and knew nothing.)

In my sophomore year we did *The Music Man* and I held dear only one truth: I was born to play Harold Hill. Yes, Robert Preston had done some nice things with the role, but my interpretation was going to illuminate the part to such an extent that the ghost of my rendition would cripple all future performances until the end of time. This did not come to pass, however, as the role went to someone else. (Fucking high school politics. The worst!) I was unceremoniously tossed in with the lumpen and spent the show laboring in the chorus, safely protected from both the glare of the footlights and the corneal tissue of the audience. I stood in the shadows, glowering as I assumed a typical Iowan townsperson might glower, and vowed to myself that this would not happen again. Next year I would be the lead in the musical.

And as it turned out, I was. We were doing *Bye Bye Birdie* and I knew with all my being that I had been placed on this sphere to play the part of Albert Peterson. My competition was fierce but I had a leg up on him; Dick Van Dyke, my friend from all of those afternoons on the hassock, had played the role of Albert originally on Broadway. I never saw Mr. Van Dyke play the part, but I channeled him during my audition and completely won over those who had condemned me not a year earlier. It was official the following day: I was Albert Peterson.

The rehearsal period was one of the happiest times of my life. I was, at the tender age of sixteen, totally on my game, getting every laugh in the script and finding three or four dozen more that I'm sure the authors themselves were unaware were there. Every rehearsal ended with the teachers shaking their heads in awe and admiration, and my fellow cast members sitting at my feet looking for advice, direction or a simple word of assurance. But then came the day when it was finally decreed that we should rehearse a certain scene near the end of the show. It was time to rehearse the kiss.

The kiss is a big thing in high school shows because, while most high school boys have kissed girls by the age of sixteen, most high school boys doing musicals have not, and in many cases never will. There was a great deal of sniggering from chorus members watching from the wings (jealous bastards!) as my co-star and I prepared for our big moment. We performed the scene and the kiss in workmanlike fashion, but I felt a touch tentative and I told my director that I wanted to rehearse the scene again. He said he needed the stage to work on another scene, but that we should feel free to go off and practice on our own. That, after a fresh cannonade of sniggering, is precisely what we did.

We practiced the scene again. It went so well that further rehearsal seemed unnecessary, but we pressed on for another hour or so. We decided to practice somewhere else after the prying eyes and flash camera of a janitor interrupted us, and we reconvened behind a bank of shelves in a dark storage closet on the second floor of the building. We practiced with great intensity for what seemed like only a half an hour or so, but when we emerged from the building we were surprised to find that night had fallen and the moon was already high in the sky. We wondered aloud as to how we were going to get home, but luckily our parents had called in separate missing persons reports, and the police gathered us up after finding us practicing some more in a lightly wooded area not half a mile from the school.

We were undeterred by this incident. In fact, it only served to strengthen our dedication to our craft. We practiced for what seemed like weeks on end, breaking only for meals and air, until finally the evening of the performance arrived. I will never forget the electricity that coursed through us all as we sat backstage getting made up. For the next few hours, the world would turn its back on the sun and revolve instead around a marginally talented group of high school students from a small coastal town in Massachusetts, and me. Places was called and I found myself alone onstage waiting for the overture to end and the curtain to rise. I was the first performer the audience would see. I would set the tone for the evening. The burden of the entire enterprise sat squarely on my sixteen-year-old shoulders.

And oh, how I sparkled! I got huge laughs right out of the gate, working the material with a surefootedness that belied my tender years. I had the audience in the palm of my hand, then in the crook of my neck and finally under the sole of my left foot, and I manipulated them from spot to spot with an ease the caliber of which was normally only acquired after twenty or so years on the Orpheum circuit. At the curtain call children rushed the stage with great bundles of daisies, women offered babies to be kissed, phone numbers to be called and keys to their homes with specific directions stating when it would be safe to come on over, and grown men sat weeping in their seats, entertained beyond all belief and questioning whether their attraction to the young man they had just seen was lasting or momentary. The evening was a complete triumph. My place in the show business firmament was all but assured.

When I arrived home after the cast party, my back sore from hundreds of hearty slaps and my ears ringing with a thousand cries of joy and congratulation, I found my mother waiting up to greet me. Smiling the smile of one who is asking a question the answer to which is already known, I queried her, "Well? What did you think?" My mother smiled lovingly, then she replied.

"I think you're going to be a writer."

And that was the first time I knew.

Peter Tolan has co-written the screenplays for *Analyze This, My Fellow Americans,* and *What Planet Are You From?* and his television writing credits include *Murphy Brown,* Billy Crystal's HBO series *Sessions, Style and Substance,* and *The Larry Sanders Show.* He won his first Emmy on *Murphy Brown* and his second Emmy for writing (with Garry Shandling) the series finale of *The Larry Sanders Show,* an episode that also won the prestigious Peabody Award. He lives in Pasadena with his wife and three children and his prestigious Peabody Award.

MICHAEL TOLKIN

THE FIRST TIME I sold anything came about six months after I got to New York from Vermont, where I'd finished college. I was changing subway lines at Columbus Circle when I ran into someone I'd known at Bard, my first school, before I dropped out. So it had been three or four years since I'd seen him. He was on his way to bet on a horse at Belmont Park, and having nothing better to do, except look for work or figure out my life, I went with him. This was early in the fall.

The beauty of a friendship with degenerates dissolves after a time into the recognition that to be friends with degenerates is degeneracy itself. One might say, for the sake of holding up talent's need for quaint experience, that a season of dissolution, contemplated from a safe distance, makes for the stuff of one's work, but dissolution shows its ravages long after we have renounced those bad days. I stayed at the track for about three or four months. If I can't quite remember when I began I can date the end of the run, a Christmas Eve at Yonkers Raceway.

At Belmont my friend demonstrated his system, a formula that used past performance and workout times, along with weight carried, all published in the *Racing Form*. Since I knew nothing about this, it seemed reasonable, and he won a few more races than he lost. I had little pocket money in those days, I was living on liverwurst and tomato sandwiches, and the Cuban Chinese restaurants that you don't see much of anymore on the Upper West Side.

This was not my first trip to the track with him. In Los Angeles, on the first round of our friendship, we had followed his sure instinct for losing his trust fund to the quarter horse track at Los Alamitos, and also to Del Mar, where we won. At Los Alamitos, we lost, and I followed my friend into the parking lot, where he begged for money. It was an odd thing, he just asked other guys for cash, saying we were tapped out, which wasn't all true, and they looked at us as one would expect, there was nothing broken about us, and I thought, we are giving the really needy a bad break here, we are draining the shallow largesse of other gamblers. But this was a friend who had lost his last girlfriend after he had talked her into starring in a soft-core dirty movie. He told me this, perhaps he was lying but it's an odd story to tell on oneself if the intention is to impress. She'd been chained between two posts against her will, and she screamed. She became a nurse, he said, years later.

I bet very little, but a few lucky trifectas gave me hundreds of dollars, and in those days that was enough for a month; it's a measure of my dumb caution that I actually saved some, and paid my rent, and bought shoes. My friend, whose parents lived at the last socially acceptable apartment building on the lower end of Park Avenue, in the fifties, always had money. He lived in near squalor on Amsterdam Avenue, in a one-bedroom apartment that smelled of wet dog.

He had a strange locution. Long after our horse lost, he would say, "If he comes in, and we bet a hundred dollars, we get . . ." and he'd calculate the winnings. This appealed to me as a good sign of insanity.

We once bought Cracker Jacks™ at the track in Atlantic City, a really pretty old track, favored by J. Edgar Hoover, and the prize was two small plastic horses with strings attached, at the end of which were weights half the size of a BB, and when you dropped the weights off the edge of a table, the horses would follow. We bet on them, but he with more ardor than I. We won at Atlantic City, on Avatar, I think, and for the first time in my life I had a shave from a barber. I knew this was all pointless, but I didn't know what else to do with my life.

On Christmas Eve we went to Yonkers Raceway, to try and make money from the trotters. It made no sense to go, since my friend had always held it as a matter of faith that the trotters were fixed, that the drivers of the sulkies worked among themselves to set up the races and that picking a winner at the trotters was a matter of coincidence only.

It was a cold night, with sleet driving the gamblers under the balconies in the grandstands. There were a few thousand men in coats, betting their children's Christmas present money. Most of them were Chinese. It was exhilarating to be among them, satisfying to know a lower depth. My friend and I lost money until the last race, when we were down to whatever one means by nothing when you have something. We bet a trifecta, and it came in, and we had twelve hundred dollars. I was saved.

I was twenty-four and made out with my friend's sixteen-year-old sister, and a friend of hers, and when I woke up in the morning saw a crease under my eye that never went away.

His parents had adopted all of their children. He was born German or Swedish, tall and blond, but he grew up with a rich Jewish grandfather who taught him some Yiddish. He liked to eat at kosher dairy restaurants, and have a boiled or poached egg with creamed spinach.

I tried writing a short story about all of this, but the simple truth didn't need the mask of fiction, so I wrote a few hundred words about my day at Atlantic City and sent it to the *Village Voice*. An editor had read something else I'd submitted once before, which they didn't print, but he encouraged me, and this time he said, "Congratulations."

I invited the editor to a party that my gambling friend knew about, and I was called from the living room into the den because the editor was feeling up a woman so drunk she was passed out on the floor, and the party's host wanted him to leave. The editor rubbed his hands on her chest and he said, "You're beautiful, it's okay."

———

The *New Yorker* called **Michael Tolkin** "an L.A. Antonioni with a sense of humor." In *Artforum* he was called "the only American filmmaker working near the level of Pasolini and Kieslowski." As a writer/director, his two films, *The Rapture* and *The New Age*, were opening-night selections at the Telluride Film Festival. As writer/producer, he is best known for *The Player*, for which he won the Writers Guild Award, the British Academy Award, the Chicago Film Critics' Award, the PEN Center USA West Literary Award, and the Edgar Allan Poe Award for best crime screenplay. He was also nominated for an Academy Award®. As one of the film's producers he was awarded the Golden

Globe, the New York Film Critics Circle Award, and the Independent Feature Project Spirit Award for best picture of the year. *The Rapture,* 1991, starring Mimi Rogers and David Duchovny, was nominated for three Spirit Awards. He has also co-written three films: the HBO movie, *The Burning Season,* starring the late Raul Julia and directed by John Frankenheimer, for which he won the Humanitas Prize and an Emmy nomination; *Deep Cover,* starring Laurence Fishburne and Jeff Goldblum; and *Deep Impact,* a Dreamworks co-production with Paramount Pictures.

In 1995, Grove Press published *The Player, The Rapture,* and *The New Age: Three Screenplays by Michael Tolkin.* His two novels, *The Player* and *Among the Dead,* have been translated and published around the world.

AUDREY WELLS

THE FIRST, and for that matter, the last time anyone said anything meaningful to me about becoming a screenwriter in Hollywood, the words of wisdom came from my friend Alan Sharp, the Scottish screenwriter and novelist. I was 25 years old, and working as Alan's assistant on a movie he had written and was directing. As a screenwriter, Alan's work habits were shocking. He wrote two scripts at a time, in longhand on legal pads, and never revised a word. His unfettered creativity filled me with longing. I wanted to write scripts, too, I told him; and the following words are the sum total of what he had to say to me on the matter:

"One day, you will sell your screenplay, and then your problems will begin."

Now that I have been a working screenwriter for over a decade, I am fully qualified to tell you that the above declaration was not a prediction, but a curse. The kind of lasting, nasty curse that witches dole out when you forget to invite them to your first-born's christening. "A curse with legs," to use industry parlance. A curse under which I have labored for the last eleven years.

Mind you, there are curses and there are curses, and there are worse things than suffering the ignominious indignities heaped upon the successful screenwriter. There are, for example, the igno-minious indignities heaped upon the unsuccessful screenwriter. Most of the latter variety occur as a direct result of sitting up in your bed in the middle of the night thinking, "Oh my God I have no money. What will I do?" The answer crawls out from under the blankets and sits on your chest wagging its tail: *anything*.

One really fun job I had when I was putting myself through grad school and starting to write was as the assistant to the direc-tor of the television commercials for Carpeteria. Carpeteria commercials were always very artistic in that they involved a scantily clad genie rolling around on wall-to-wall carpeting. The director's office was conveniently located underground, in a basement apartment in Hollywood. My first job was to "find the awful smell." It didn't take long.

My stint with the Carpeteria auteur, while odoriferous, was not for nought, as shortly thereafter I was offered work directing a superstar, an international icon. Never mind that she was nine inches long and plastic. My job, at Mattel, was to pose Barbie for her industrial videos. Barbie loves her new outfit! Arms high! Barbie relaxes in her whirlpool. Legs up! Barbie gets into her pink Corvette. Ooops! Barbie fell down. Oh, well. To this day, she remains the most compliant actress I have ever worked with.

But lest you get the impression that shit jobs are easy to come by in Hollywood, let me say that even lowly employment was often beyond my reach. I remember begging the owner of Miracle Films to give me a job as an apprentice editor. Miracle Films made porn movies. Their slogan was, "Miracle Films: If it's a good film, it's a miracle." The Big Guy with the pinkie ring wouldn't give me the job. For some reason, I brought out the father/protector in him. "What's a nice girl like you doing in a place like this?" was basically his question. Starving, I wanted to tell him. Starving and desperate for work.

Clearly, I needed a better way to make a living. It was time to try and write a script and sell it. But what should I write about?

During this time in my life, I was fortunate enough to have a twice-yearly consulting job that took me far, far away from Los Angeles. It took me, to be more precise, to remote native villages in the Alaskan arctic, where I taught broadcasting workshops at tiny, dilapidated radio stations. The job had unparalleled perks. I got to fly over glaciers in single-prop planes, stay at the Thunderbird Hotel and Laundromat, eat at Pepe's Top of the World Cafe, which boasted the world's northernmost Mexican food, and watch the northern lights dance over the broadcast towers of the radio stations I worked at. The Corporation for Public Broadcasting funded the workshops, and the point was for me to encourage the Inuit and Yupik residents to participate in and work at their own radio stations. People would shyly put on headphones for the first time in their lives, look at the microphone with suspicion, and then leap out of their seats with surprise at the sound of their own voices. I remember working with a young woman who came into the studio wearing a large parka. Every time she spoke into the microphone, I heard a strange, muffled cooing sound, in harmony with her voice. After a while I looked so perplexed that she exploded into giggles, and pulled the zipper of her parka down to reveal the source of the sound: a baby snuggled against her breast.

It was on the return flight from one of these trips north that I looked out the window at the impossibly beautiful Alaska Range, and the obvious finally occurred to me: What if I wrote about this? What if there was a girl, like me but not like me, from L.A., who goes to Alaska to get a radio station back on the air, who's a fish out of water, who thinks she'll teach them something, but they really teach her something, blah, blah, blah?

I came home, wrote the script, and called it *Radio Free Alaska*. I gave it to my dear friend Tyler Bensinger, and he gave it to his agent, and she gave it to two women producers, and they gave it to Paramount, and Paramount bought it, and everybody said "Yippee! You made it!" and the check came, and I was no longer broke, and I was very, very relieved.

Until the curse kicked in.

Here is how my problems began: Because I was a "first-time writer," the producers had no long-term commitment to me, and after I fulfilled my contractual obligation for a second draft, they took me to lunch and fired me over the salad course. One of my producers, feeling perhaps that I might want to get a jump on my solitary suffering, told me that I needn't stay through the main course, if I would rather go home and cry. I will never forget her consideration.

After those two nice ladies tanked me, they hired a procession of more successful screenwriters who rewrote me. Not all rewriters damage scripts, but I was not so lucky. In the case of *Radio Free Alaska*, the rewriters changed the Inuit characters' names to "funny Injun" names, and basically did for Native characters what Stepin Fetchit did for African Americans. At one point, the

producers called me back and confessed to me that they knew
the rewriters had destroyed the script, and would I like to come
back in, quietly, for no money, and rewrite the rewriters, under
their names, to make *their* draft of *my* script look better than it
was, so that the studio would still be interested in my now
butchered project when the rewrite came in. I declined. After all,
you have to learn to say no.

Eleven years later, *Radio Free Alaska* still sits on a shelf at
Paramount, and usually I forget that it's there. I've had four of
my scripts made into films, one with me as the director, and for
the most part, I've left the highly encumbered *Radio Free* behind.
I admit that now and then I think about that girl with the baby
under her parka, and I feel a pang—I would truly love to bring
her to life on screen someday.

And maybe I will. After all, screenplays have legendary shelf
lives. I picture long, dark corridors with endless shelves contain-
ing thousands of laboratory jars filled with formaldehyde. And in
each jar floats an unproduced screenplay, yellowing and odd,
waiting for reanimation.

Aspiring screenwriters, I hand down the curse:

One day, you will sell your screenplay. And then your problems will begin.

Audrey Wells worked as a radio journalist before obtaining her masters in film from UCLA. Since
then, she has written numerous original screenplays, including *The Kid, The Truth About Cats &
Dogs,* and (as co-writer) *George of the Jungle.* In 1999, Audrey wrote and directed the independent feature film *Guinevere,* which received the award for Best Screenplay at the Sundance Film
Festival and the Jury Prize from the Deauville Film Festival.

RICHARD WESLEY

THE FIRST TIME I ever saw a film based on a script I had written appear on a screen occurred back in the spring of 1974 with the opening of *Uptown Saturday Night*. I'd written that for Sidney Poitier and First Artists Pictures. I came to Sidney Poitier a moderately successful playwright in New York, with several off-Broadway productions and a Drama Desk Award under my belt. He needed a writer to turn an idea he had for a film comedy into a script. I was a young man who was always used to taking his time putting ideas onto a printed page, editing them, shaping them one way and then another, experimenting, discarding or keeping my ideas as the situation warranted. The process could be time-consuming but they were my ideas and it was my time. What I learned, working with Sidney, was that all of this would have to change. I was going into a collaborative situation, one in which cooperation, patience and adherence to deadline became increasingly important. The independence I enjoyed off-Broadway gave way to interdependence. Time, which had always been just another part of the landscape, now became my taskmaster. I even had to learn to redefine myself. In the theater I was an artist; in the motion picture industry, I was the "writer"—a cog in a much larger machine. In the theater, my place, my dignity was assured. In the motion picture industry, nothing is assured and dignity is something fought for, tooth and nail, under assault from so many quarters every day.

I'm the stronger for it, thank God. I came to understand, more clearly than ever, the DISCIPLINE of writing. And I learned to appreciate SPEED. I learned to appreciate the difference between stage dialogue and motion picture dialogue. Over time, I learned to trust the camera, as well as my actors, and to hone my dialogue accordingly. Today, I write motion picture and television scripts far more quickly than I ever wrote any of my plays—and, skillwise, I'm the better for it.

Arguments can be made that there are a lot of people in the business who don't care about writers, don't give a damn about scripts and treat us with thinly veiled contempt. But, there are many more people (yes, some of them are directors) who do care, and who go out of their way to demonstrate their concern for our craft and their appreciation of our professionalism. Sidney Poitier was one of those people. I'm fortunate that he was my gateway into this business. I'm in a position, now, to be of assistance to new writers who are just coming into the business. It is my hope that I can be there to make their "first time" as thrilling, exciting and as professional as mine was all those years ago.

Richard Wesley's professional writing career began in earnest in 1971 with the staging of his Drama Desk Award–winning political drama *The Black Terror* at Joseph Papp's Public Theater. An accomplished playwright, he has also written extensively for film and television. His feature film credits include *Uptown Saturday Night, Let's Do It Again, Fast Forward,* and *Native Son;* his television credits include *The House of Dries Dear* (PBS), *Murder Without Motive* (NBC), and *Mandela and DeKlerk* (Showtime). Mr. Wesley is currently associate professor of playwriting and screenwriting in the Dramatic Writing Program at the Tisch School of the Arts, New York University, and serves on the Executive Council of the Writers Guild of America, east.

STEVEN ZALLIAN

THE FIRST TIME the phone rang it wasn't for me, it was for some guy at the bar. He was using Barney's for his office, too, and the pay phone by the men's room for his calls. This was a while ago. Before cell phones. Before pagers. Before they made Barney's take down the "No Fags Allowed" sign out front.

The call I was waiting for would be from my first, and only, agent, Harold Greene. He would be calling to tell me which of the two companies he had bidding against each other for my script wanted it more. At least that's what he told me earlier. What I feared, as I sat with my friend at Barney's waiting, was that he would push both of them too far, to the point where neither one of them would really want it at all.

I hardly knew Harold. I had only met him the week before. I had given my script to several agents—dropping it off and watching their receptionists set it on the floor behind their desks already awash with others—but he was the only one who bothered reading it.

His office was on the corner of La Cienega and Waring on the third floor of a white stucco building, "get off the elevator, turn left, end of the hall." There was a small sign with straightforward lettering next to the door: "Eisenbach, Greene, Duchow."

I remember the things in his office, and would watch them over the course of the next several years move with him from this office to a smaller, less cheerful one on Beverly across from Jay's Coffee Shop, and then to the apartment in Marina del Rey that he shared with his wife, Marilyn. From the window of that one, you could watch moored sailboats bob in the water.

He had a hand-painted lead soldier on his desk. And a stack of little magnetic figures you could arrange like acrobats, but never keep from falling over. He had two black pens that sat in brass swivel holders on a weighted leather base, one of which I used to sign our first contract together. On the wall behind where he sat, he had a painting of an old train you looked at when you talked to him. On the wall behind you, there was a framed adage someone had given him, in calligraphy script, that he could see when he talked to you. More than once he would ask, "Did you ever read that?" You would say, "Yes." And he would say, "I love that."

Harold was of the Old School. He drove a big American car, a black Cadillac Seville, and had trouble keeping up with the New School, the young agents, Ovitz and CAA and all the rest taking over. He took me to lunch in it the day we met, to a place on Sunset that isn't there anymore, called the Cock & Bull.

The Cock & Bull, I suppose, was meant to resemble an English pub. It had no windows that I can remember, like a lot of places that aren't around anymore. Now it's all glass and light in restaurants. The Cock & Bull and its clientele favored smoky darkness and heavy steaks and cocktails in the middle of the day.

Harold told me about the old days. Of course, I never dreamed that these would ever become the old days, sitting with him in that room that was so dark you could barely see each other. But the old days he was talking about were the thirties and forties, when he was just starting out, under contract to the studios, a young screenwriter in a town that no longer exists any more than the Cock & Bull.

He told me he would only be sending my script out to a select group. "No reason to paper the town." The truth was, the town was changing so fast it was hard for him to keep track of who was who. The "select" group, I would understand later, were two guys Harold's age, producers still in business from the old days, men he knew personally, who, like him, still drank cocktails at lunch.

Harold had them bidding against each other into the night as I waited for his call at Barney's Beanery. The next time the pay phone rang it was for me. "Are you sitting down?" he asked. "I can't sit down, the phone is bolted to the wall." I couldn't hear him all that well either, with all the noise from the bar, when he said, "Order yourself a drink. You are now a professional writer."

Harold and I stayed together for the next twenty years, over the course of which his client list grew smaller and smaller until there was only me. He is now, I believe, 85. His wife, Marilyn, died a few years ago. Not long after the funeral, he blacked out in his Cadillac late one night, crashed into a tree and woke up two days later in intensive care at UCLA Medical Center. He's been in and out of the hospital ever since, and now, when at home, requires around-the-clock nursing care.

The last time I saw him there, we sat in his office and talked. He wasn't hearing so well, even in the quiet of the marina in the middle of the week, the water lapping against the sailboat hulls. I toyed with the acrobat magnets on his desk, trying to get them all to stand on each other's shoulders, knowing I wouldn't be able to, having tried and failed a hundred times before, and repeated, when he said, "What?" the thing I had come to tell him that neither one of us wanted to hear.

When I finally got up to leave, as he was watching me go for the last time, he said, "Oh, by the way, have you ever read that?" pointing to the framed adage with the calligraphy script, hanging on the wall by the door. "I love that," he said. Of course, I had read it. I had read it countless times. I knew it by heart, but I read it again, for him. It said, "God, I know you will provide. But will you provide *until* you provide?"

———————

Steven Zallian received an Academy Award® for his screenplay *Schindler's List*. His work on the film was also honored with a Writers Guild Award, a Golden Globe, a BAFTA Award, and the Humanitas Prize. His other screenwriting credits include *Awakenings, Clear and Present Danger, Jack the Bear,* and *The Falcon and the Snowman*. He also wrote the screenplays for and directed *Searching for Bobby Fischer* and *A Civil Action* and is currently writing *The Duke of Deception,* which he will also direct. He was born in Fresno, California, and was raised in Los Angeles. He attended Sonoma State College and graduated from San Francisco State University.

THE WRITERS GUILD FOUNDATION

The Writers Guild Foundation was established in 1966 as a nonprofit charitable corporation by a group of television and motion picture writers, members of the Writers Guild of America, west. The founding president was James. R. Webb.

The Foundation's mission is:

- to promote and encourage excellence in writing;
- to educate the public concerning the role of the writer in film and television;
- to preserve the work of film and television writers and thereby to create a significant historical resource for future generations;
- to encourage the further education of writers; and
- to promote communication between writers.

The Foundation's current major programs include:

- The James R. Webb Memorial Library, housing over 4,000 award-nominated scripts and a reference collection of books, tapes, and photographs related to writers and writing, and to the history of writers in Hollywood;

- The Writer Speaks, a series of oral history interviews on video with the great writers of film and television;
- Words, a short film highlighting and celebrating the writer's contribution to some of the great moments in motion pictures;
- Educational seminars and tributes, including its annual Career Achievement Award;
- An academic liaison program with schools and colleges;
- A joint-venture script publishing project; and
- Conferences and international exchanges, including Words Into Pictures.

The Foundation's activities are funded by voluntary contributions from writers and industry friends.

For more information, please contact:

Writers Guild Foundation
7000 West Third Street
Los Angeles, CA 90048-4329
Telephone: 323-782-4692